RSO Advocacy

Magazine

Produced by RSO-Advocacy.org

Representing the more than 750,000 registered offenders,
their families and friends.

RSO Advocacy Magazine, a biannual print magazine, published by RSO Advocacy with distribution worldwide.

RSO Advocacy Staff

Managing Director	Randy English	r.english@rso-advocacy.org
Interviewer	Kate Logan	k.logan@rso-advocacy.org
Production Coordinator	Al Lynne	allynne@rso-advocacy.org
Chief Editor	E.D.Tory	
Researcher/Writer	Will Bass	will_bass@rso-advocacy.org
Writer	Alan Davis	alan@rso-advocacy.org
Writer	H. Neimand	h.niemand@rso-advocacy.org
Website Management	Nick Maietta	nick@rso-advocacy.org
Advertising information	Randy English	r.english@rso-advocacy.org
Letters to the Editor		postmaster@rso-advocacy.org
Website		www.rso-advocacy.org

What is
RSO Advocacy?

We are a group of dedicated reform activists, some seasoned veterans and some new to the reform movement. We recognize that there is an ongoing escalation of legislative, judicial, and law enforcement agencies comprised of local, county, state and federal bodies of government who campaign for increased legislation primarily restricting the Constitutional rights of offenders that have completed their confinement to prison, probation or parole.

The very same legislation that appears – seemingly on the surface, to be protecting children and their families is not at all the case. In fact, the ongoing assault depriving RSO's of their civil rights, after serving their punishment as determined by the court system, not only affects the children and families of the community at large, but, indeed affects the RSO's children and their families as well.

At RSO Advocacy, we seek to bring about awareness of issues that the public and even some in the reform movement shies away from. In doing so, we hope that the public will become informed and demand better and more effective laws. Laws based on common sense and science, not purely emotion driven.

Our goals in part are:

1. Promote only effective laws that serve all those concerned and involved with sex offender legislation and it's affects on all children, all families, all of our communities – particularly our legal system – our court system and all other related areas of concern.

2. Promote common sense laws that reflect scientific studies and research data by those professionals educated in the fields of sex offender research, offender rehabilitation, offender law and punishment, offender education etc.

3. Encompass all and any resources available that will help to support RSO Advocacy to educate ourselves and others by developing a clearer understanding of the dynamics involved in recognizing behavior relating to re-committing a sex offense. Not only by the offender, but by those persons who could become a victim of a sex offense or others who may be in a position to concern themselves with behavior of an individual that may reflect uncommon behavior relating to sexual behavior.

4. RSO Advocacy is also concerned with vigilante activity that has caused the registry to become a public "hit list." These unlawful acts have left a trail of murder victims; some innocent bystanders and some whose crimes were 10 or more years in the past and have been living a "model" life. Additionally, we are dramatically concerned over news journalists reporting methods, which promote public hysteria simply to gain ratings. For example – manipulating or leaving out facts regarding a sex offense by second guessing the facts and placing a slanted story to the public or reporting a recidivism study and stating a misleading or even patently false numbers.

We fervently believe that change to a more common sense approach to sex offender issues is imperative. As it now stands, legislation that has been enacted against registered sex offenders and upheld in the courts has become case law. What does that mean? It means that these same laws and law principles can and will be used against others....anyone that the government sees fit to exercise these same restrictions against; no matter what that offense is. Examples are DUI, Arson, Animal Abuse, Child Abuse, Murder and the list goes on and on. Many of these registers have already been proposed and some states, like Hawaii, have already added registries for classifications other than the sex offenders

We invite you to join us on this journey into the heart of the problem, while we seek practical and effective solutions that work for everyone, with the ultimate goal of stopping sexual abuse in all of its ugly forms. ∎

Table of Contents

Article	Author	Page
What was That Question?	Randy English	2
A Child is Sexually Abused	Al Lynne	4
We're on the Regisrty	Randy English	5
Shaming Punishment	Will Bass	7
Burdens of Innocence	Randy English	8
Internet is not a Babysitter!	Randy English	9
Advocating for All	Allan Davis	11
Vicki Henry Interview	Randy English and Kate Logan	12
The Sex Offender Era	Al Lynne	15
Recidivism Numbers	Will Bass	18
Vigilantism	Randy English	20
Reflections of History - 2010	Randy English	21
Reflections of History - 2012	Randy English	23
Brace For Impact	Al Lynne	25
Seperation of Powers	Will Bass	27
A World in Chaos	Randy English	28
Where has our Freedom Gone?	Robert Wolfe	30
Former Sex Offenders and Employment	Randy English	34
100,000 Unregistered Sex Offenders	Randy English	35
Food For Thought	Penn Greene	36
If It Saves Just One Child	H. Niemand	41
Open Letter to SCOTUS	An Offender	38
Cover Story - **The Gary Blanton Story**	Randy English and Kate Logan	42
Hacker to Hacker	Nicholas Maietta	46
Supreme Court Received False Info	Will Bass and Al Lynne	48
Sexting Laws	Randy English	50
Self Serving Politicians	Will Bass	54
Silence of Offenders	Penn Greene	55
Would You Consider it Punishment	Lynn Gilmore	56
Community Notification	Robert Wolfe	57
No Worse Than a Drivers License	E.D.Tory	61
The Problem of Recidivsm	RSO Adovcacy Staff	63
RSOA Contract	RSO Advocacy Staff	64
Skew the Numbers	Will Bass	65
Fortune Telling	Will Bass	66
Overkill	Randy English	69
Reggie O'Fender Part 1		70
Mortal Slur	Al Lynne	71
Registry, Punishment by Default	Will Bass and Al Lynne	72

What was that Question?

by Randy English

When you hear reports that say 8 out of 10 children are solicited for sex on-line, have you ever asked, who those victims are, and how do we know this is true?

Sure you know who the perpetrator is, don't you? It's some old guy sitting at a computer cruising the net for another victim. But who are the victims?

The victims are mostly teenagers. They are in chat rooms or on other social media and someone will pop up and ask if they want to "hook up", or offer "sexting" and some just straight out ask for sex.

So, when, in an interview situation, the question, "Have you ever been solicited on-line for sex?" comes up, what is the answer? 8 out of 10 children answered yes.

I wish that there was a follow up question to this...Wait there is! According to the Department of Justice, the average age of that old perpetrator, is a whopping 14 years old. You see, when we hear statistics about, sex offenses, that are only partially quoted, our mind always goes to the negative side. We are inclined to be open to suggestion. This is why advertising is so effective. All it takes is a little suggestion and our mind does the rest. But in this instance our minds led us to a false conclusion. While it is true that 8 out of 10 children are solicited for sex on-line, the perpetrator is not an old man, it is a young teen, and it's not just the boys asking to hook up. Today girls are highly sexually active and are more aggressive than in past decades. So before you think of little Sissy in pigtails, look at MTV during Spring Break. Do you really think that those 19 and 20 year olds just became uninhibited? Don't fool yourself. That took a lot of time. Girls just don't all-of-a-sudden pull their top off in front of thousands of people they don't know. That process started way back, according to the DOJ, when they were around 14 years old.

If there were other follow up questions I would like to ask; "Did you know the person that solicited you?" and "Was this person from your school/neighborhood?"

If we could add the answers to these question into the statistics, the final conclusion would be that very few, likely in the 0.000% range have been solicited by an old predator on-line. Now if we go one step further and add Registered Sex Offenders into this mix, because according to society, they are the greatest threat. If we add them in, guess what, the number of children solicited by a registered sex offender on-line would be so low that you would have a better chance of being struck by lighting-three days in a row.

So, what was that question? That question was misleading. It was designed to shock you, to make you angry, so that you would react. Did you react? If you reacted in the desired way, you were a victim of smooth marketing. Learn the facts before you react! ∎

Can you point out the Registered Sex Offender?

Fact: Registered Sex Offenders can be both male or female and range from 9 years old and up!

A Child is Sexually Abused Every Two Minutes

by Al Lynne

It has been said that a child is sexually abused every two minutes. This is the position many proponents take when they present an article for their cause. When this one was searched on the Internet, it was pretty much fill in the blank, because there is no consistency in numbers, there are no reliable resources and even if there were, it would be next to impossible to prove. Another one says one in three girls and one in five boys will be sexually abused before they reach the age of eighteen. Again, there are no reliable resources and even if there were, it would be next to impossible to prove. The arguments from both sides, each have valid points. Child Sexual Abuse is a problem and it truly needs to be addressed. Child Sexual Abuse can and should be reduced, if not completely eliminated. Child Sexual Abuse is damaging to a child because children, both pre- and post- pubescent, have minds which are immature to sexual activity and that innocence is vital and it has a self protective and instinctive mental guard, which naturally prevents them from premature sexual activity. Once this boundary is broken, and a child discovers sexuality, that innocence is lost and that mental security no longer has its self-protective capabilities. This is why it is so vital for parents to be well educated with the facts regarding Child Sexual Abuse and know the reliable statistics along with how to prevent their children from being abused and abusing others. Our greatest enemy on the front lines of the battle against Child Sexual Abuse is ignorance. If we ignore the facts and if we ignore our Children, then we expose ourselves to a risk that one of our own children could be the next victim. This is why it is important to verify any statistical information, making sure it is scientifically sound. If the information prompts us to fear, or has emotional influence, more than likely it is manipulated information and shouldn't be believed, used, or considered. It may be from the sponsor of an ad for a product to buy, or it could just be the latest propaganda tactic. It is more important to do your own research because a sponsor is more interested in selling you a product than they are for yours, or ANY other child's health and well being. ∎

Do you trust the person in charge of instructing your children?

Over 99% of all new sex crimes are commited by someone who is NOT on the registry.

WE ARE ON THE REGISTRY!

BY RANDY ENGLISH

The Sex Offender Registry. Just saying the words makes most people cringe. It evokes the thought of some fat, old, white guy in a dirty tank-top, peering out from behind a bush, ready to jump on the first kid that comes by. But this is not reality. Today the registry lists people of all ages, including children as young as 9 years old. They come from every walk of life, every religious background, every social status and every ethnicity. And they are not all men. But the registry includes far more than this. What else does it include?

When someone is placed on the registry, they must hand over a lot of personal information, even some things that most people would consider private information. The obvious is their address. Then there is the make, model and color of their car and the license plate number. Some states even offer the personalized plate with the much coveted Sex Offender label on it. Other things that a person must hand over are work addresses and internet identifiers.

The Whole Family is Registered

Now imagine for a moment that you're a twelve-year-old child and one of your parents is on the registry. How will this affect you? In today's modern world, most people have the internet so your friends will soon find out. Better yet is when the police come to your school or even to your neighbors and tell all of your friends families. You will be a *laughing-stock. You will be shunned. You will see them pointing and talking behind your back. It may get so bad that your consider suicide.

What if you're the spouse of the registered offender? How would that affect you? If you have a family car and your spouse drives that car, your car is registered. And if you have those snazzy sex offender license plates you will get a lot of attention. After all, those people think you're on the registry, well you are. You will be hated, called names; you may receive some physical abuse, perhaps sexual advances. But one thing is for sure, you won't have a normal life.

If you or a family member were on the registry you would have another fear as well. Vigilantism is on the increase. The murders of registered offenders is more common that you may think. Harassment and vandalism are daily occurrences.

If you or a family member were on the registry, how would the police react if you were threatened, harassed or if your home or car were vandalized? They often treat it as trivial, frivolous and petty... You could be told, *"You will be fine there is nothing to worry about."* But you would know that is not true. That fear and anxiety you feel is not trivial, frivolous or petty, it is quite real and deserves justice and protection or at the least some professional courtesy like any other tax paying citizen would receive. But you won't get it. ∎

"The age of the phrase may be the reason that it is often linked with the practice of putting people into stocks as a punishment. The stocks were a means of punishment in use at the time the phrase was coined, by which people were tortured or ridiculed. Victims were held by having their ankles, and occasionally the wrists too, trapped in holes between two sliding boards. The punishment, although not as harsh as the pillory, in which people were confined by the neck, was severe and certainly not intended to be humorous." http://www.phrases.org.uk/meanings/laughing-stock.html

There are now over 750,00 registered former offenders in the United States. How many family members do you think there are that are dealing with the effects of the registry? It won't be long before political leaders find out. How do you think they will vote?

Anouncements

ST. PAUL, Minn. -- A federal judge has certified a lawsuit challenging the constitutional ity of the Minnesota Sex Offender Program as a class action on behalf of everyone committed to the program.

U.S. District Judge Donovan Frank ruled Tuesday that the lawsuit meets the legal requirements to be certified as a class action. He pointed out that the proposed class includes about 600 people who've been indefinitely committed to the program, and he concluded that addressing each case individually would be an enormous drain on legal resources.

Frank writes that they all face an identical process for treatment and possible release. He says they all raise similar allegations of a lack of realistic opportunities for earning their freedom. And says they all have sufficiently similar legal interests for their cases to go forward together.

Read more here: http://www.sacbee.com/2012/07/24/4656607/judge-certifies-sex-offender-suit.html#storylink=cpy

Do you have an event you would like us to list? Contact us today. There is no cost for listing events. postmaster@rso-advocacy.org

Shaming Punishment

Shaming as a form of punishment as defined by the Court cases of People v. Meyer - People v. Lowe, 606 N.E.2d. - People v. Molz, 113 N.E.2d - People v. Johnson 528 N.E.2d - State v. Burdin 924 S.W.2d - People v. Letterlough 655 N.E.2d - Lindsay v. State 606 So. 2D.

While a conviction for a crime may extinguish a person's rights to be free and confine that person to a 8 x 10 cell For periods of 14 to 18 hours a day our Constitution guarantees as part of the Eighth Amendment. Part of the Eighth Amendment prohibition on cruel and unusual punishments says that prisoners in the custody of the State who are being punished have a right to be safe from other inmates and to receive care including medical care at the cost to the State because they are in the custody of the State and cannot take care of themselves. It is the State's responsibility to make sure that these prisoners are safe and cared for while in custody.

Since the legislature has chosen to notify the communities of the presence of registrants, and the result of that notification is shaming and vigilantism within the community, would this not oblige the state to make sure that the results of their legislation does not cause physical or emotional harm to the registrant or their families?

It would seem that creating laws to make registrants protected under hate crime legislation would be a start. Next would be to create balanced laws that allow registrants to find work and housing so they can provide for themselves and their families. Since legislators have created registries and have led to unintended consequences, it is time to eliminate those consequences.■

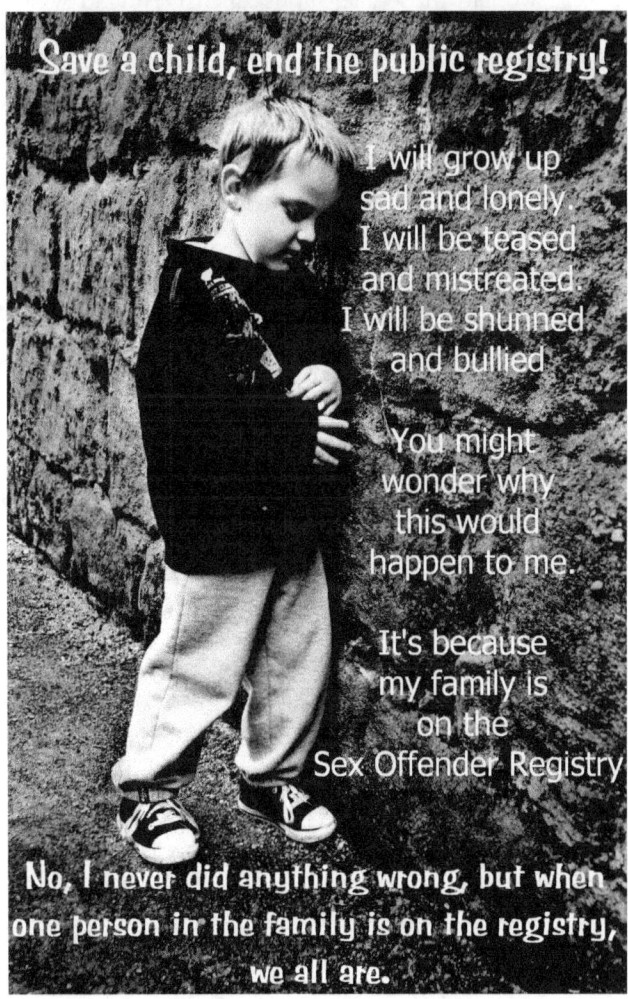

Save a child, end the public registry!

I will grow up sad and lonely. I will be teased and mistreated. I will be shunned and bullied

You might wonder why this would happen to me.

It's because my family is on the Sex Offender Registry

No, I never did anything wrong, but when one person in the family is on the registry, we all are.

THE BURDENS OF INNOCENCE

BY RANDY ENGLISH

While the nation is focused on the sexual abuse case of Jerry Sandusky, which is leading most people to believe that every sex offender is the same, an important case in Texas is barely making the news.

Michael Trevino has spent the last 22 years on the sex offender registry. But unlike Sandusky, Trevino was actually innocent and wrongly convicted. However, up until a short time ago, people could or would not have ever believed it possible.

The original court documents show that in May of 1990 a woman made allegations against Trevino which stated that her daughter had been sexually assaulted. The then eight-year-old reported that the incident had happened when she was in kindergarten and said that Trevino threatened to kill her if she told her mother. Doctors examined the child and reported finding evidence of sexual abuse.

For most people this was clearly an open and shut case. "Why would the child lie? Children never lie about such things!" You hear this all the time from child advocate groups. But they are absolutely wrong. Children can and do lie, and for Michael Trevino, it took a full 22 years for the truth to come out. In 2010, the victim recanted her story, and said: "it was another man."

It took two more years for the "system" to correct itself. On May 24, 2012 the charges against Trevino were dismissed and his name was removed from the sex offender registry.

However, this is not the end of the story. Mr. Trevino, a truly innocent man, is still listed on non-government-sanctioned sex offender sites like Homefacts.com and Sexoffender.com among others. The public should be aware that these websites are actually for-profit websites; they are not for the protection of children, or accuracy of actual facts. These websites are purely for profit.

While the public at large will not care about this news story, they actually should. The sex offender registry is filled with people who pose no danger to the public. From the wrongly convicted to Romeo and Juliet offenders, and many others who made one time mistakes, the registry is bloated with more than enough misinformation to give the public a false sense of security.

Who is really benefiting from the registry? Surely not the public. It is websites and organizations (even prisons) that have capitalized from the multi-billion dollar per year sex offender industry.

While the public sees everyone accused as being like Sandusky, the facts prove them wrong. Only a very small percentage of sex offenders fall into that particular category and most of them are in prison.

True, you will hear Legislators, the media, and others who claim to be experts, making blanket statements to the contrary. The facts, through clinical research do not support their misinformation.

Another point of this story is the lengthy amount of time, excessive cost and lack of regulations for a person to possibly clear their name; even when a victim recants. There should be a simple, effective way for those wrongly convicted to approach our court system, at any time, with new evidence, victim recantation or anything else that would possibly clear their name.

However there is no such system in place. While a prosecutor can make a rush to judgment, ruining a person's life, the innocent have little or no hope of ever getting the "system" to hear them once they are convicted. We feel it's long overdue to demand that Legislators draft legislation that will make it easier for those wrongly convicted to bring forth new evidence and as part of that same system, a fast-track to freedom for those who can prove their innocence. This should include those wrongly convicted of any sex offenses. Just as Politicians and Legislators push to appear "Tough On Crime", there should be zero tolerance for any innocent person to endure the burdens related to a Sex Crime conviction.

We wish Mr. Trevino the very best. We hope that he will sue Homefacts.com and the other "vigilante" for-profit websites which are still incorrectly listing his name as a child molester. He also deserves full compensation for the 22 years of misery he wrongfully endured as a registered sex offender.

Lastly, we hope that he will contact Legislators both in Texas and also nationally, demanding that they draft legislation to help all of those who are wrongly convicted. ■

The Internet is NOT a Babysitter!

by Randy English

For decades now the Television has been called "the babysitter". Child advocacy groups warned that many programs on Television were unfit for children and that watching too much Television was detrimental in many ways. According to several scientific studies, watching TV for prolonged periods of time has a negative effect over the intellectual development of children and leads to deterioration of the mental capacity in older people by causing both attention and memory problems in the long term.

However, for the most part, parents did not listen to the experts and today we have a large group of over-weight, anti-social, disrespectful teenagers.

Now there is a new babysitter, one that goes everywhere with children. It's called the Internet. It's in computers, phones, the TV and even in cars. It seems that today you can't get away from it nor do without it. But should it be considered a babysitter? No, it should not. If we thought that the TV would rot our kids minds, we had no idea what was coming. The Internet puts everything right at your child's fingers. I mean "everything".

Do you remember when TV got so bad that we installed parental control locks to protect Junior and Sissy? Well, today the Internet has things like that, but as I found out, kids today are some of the best computer hackers in the world. It takes them only a few minutes to find ways around these programs. So don't think you did some great service by installing them. They are almost worthless if your child wants to get around them.

With *sexting and *child porn becoming such a big issue for teens and even preteens, some parents have opted out of Internet service on their children's cell phones. At the same time, they are moving computers with Internet access into the living-room where Internet activity can be monitored much more easily. True, this may lead to some anger from your children, but given that sexting and child porn are illegal, the safety of your children are well worth the arguments that will certainly arise.

Parents must stop expecting the government to raise their children. That expectation has led to many laws that are now landing children in jail, prison, or on probation and then on the sex offender registry. Parents must one again reclaim responsibility for raising their own children. Shut off the TV, turn off the computer and sit down and get to know your child. Ask them questions and answer their questions. Really communicate with them. Talk with your children about important subjects, let them know you care. Most of all, remember the internet is not a babysitter, it is a tool that has death dealing parts that were never meant for children.■

For more information on how Sexting and Child Porn could cause your child the be placed on the sex offender registry, look for the article, "Sexting and Child Porn Laws-Their Affects on Children." in this issue of RSO Advocacy Magazine.

I can stand brute force, but brute reason is quite unbearable. There is something unfair about its use. It is hitting below the intellect."

Oscar Wilde

"Morality cannot be legislated."

Randy English

"I believe that banking institutions are more dangerous to our liberties than standing armies. Already they have raised up a moneyed aristocracy that has set the government at defiance. The issuing power should be taken from the banks and restored to the people, to whom it properly belongs."

Thomas Jefferson

"Americans [have] the right and advantage of being armed, unlike the citizens of other countries whose governments are afraid to trust their people with arms.

JAMES MADISON

"You have rights antecedent to all earthly governments; rights that cannot be repealed or restrained by human laws; rights derived from the Great Legislator of the Universe"

John Adams

"The strength of the Constitution lies entirely in the determination of each citizen to defend it. Only if every single citizen feels duty bound to do his share in this defense are the constitutional rights secure."

Albert Einstein

"The Constitution shall never be construed to prevent the people of the United States, who are peaceable citizens from keeping their own arms . . ."

SAMUEL ADAMS

"The Constitution of most of our states (and of the United States) assert that all power is inherent in the people; that they may exercise it by themselves; that it is their right and duty to be at all times armed and that they are entitled to freedom of person, freedom of religion, freedom of property, and freedom of press."

Thomas Jefferson

"I believe there are more instances of the abridgment of the freedom of the people by gradual and silent encroachments of those in power than by violent and sudden usurpations."

James Madison

We the people are the rightful masters of both Congress and the courts, not to overthrow the Constitution but to overthrow the men who pervert the Constitution."

Abraham Lincoln

"FREEDOM OF THE PRESS IS LIMITED TO THOSE WHO OWN ONE."

A.J. LIEBLING

"Don't interfere with anything in the Constitution. That must be maintained, for it is the only safeguard of our liberties."

Abraham Lincoln

Advocating for All

by Alan Davis

There is a real problem in our movement, when some decide that their crime, or some crimes, are not "as bad" as others. I hear of the no contact, or "victimless" crimes of looking at or trading child porn, the tree wetters or the Romeo/Juliet cases being different than those "contact crimes". Some in our movement want all offenders in these groups released from the registry and then believe, like the population in general, that all the rest are the "worst of the worst". Once the laws are changed to let their loved ones free, "those who should have never been put on the registry in the first place" than who cares what they do to the rest. There is, even within our own members, a feeling that "they" deserve it even if it is unconstitutional.

So, even I, can slip into this mold, thinking about those who use a weapon or violence in the commission of their crime, and even more, when someone commits a second offense. But let's look at those who's crime involved a "child". First and foremost, this does make up nearly half of all on the registry, but like all others, no two are exactly the same, and as a group, they are no more the same as the present group of all those who are on the registry.

Obviously, nearly all Romeo/Juliet cases fall into this category. Here often the problem is a question of age of consent and just as often, age of responsibility. More than half of all youth in the US are now sexual active prior to the age of consent. What makes a crime of this though is when one of the partners becomes old enough to be held responsible as an adult.

When it is reported that by the age of 18, six out of ten girls and three out of ten boys have been "sexually abused", what is being counted is all sexual activity and from these same studies,

it is discovered that the average age of the "abuser" is 14 1/2.

But there is also a great number of offenses that involve children, where the abuser is definitely an adult. Most often this occurs within the family or through very close associations. In the majority of these cases, where incest is the primary crime, there is wrong mental thinking going on where the abuser doesn't understand that what they are doing is not showing love, but is hurting the child by taking away that child's innocence. In the majority of these cases, these same abusers were abused themselves as children, and while that doesn't excuse what they are doing, it lets us understand some of the mental conditions that leads to this crime being repeated generation after generation. What is most important to understand in this type of adult on child sexual abuse, is that once it is brought out into the light, it can be addressed and will in most cases, never be repeated and thus break the cycle of abuse. There are many professionals in the Sexual Abuser Treatment field which can testify to this fact.

Prior to most of our current sex offender laws, these types of abuses were considered "the family secret", yet we're often addressed through therapy. Families were kept intact and all parties were healed. Only in the past twenty years has this type of abuse been forced by law to require reporting and criminal punishment. Families are destroyed and most all are forced into a victim mind-set for life; not only the victim, but often the abuser as well.

If this entire group of incest type of abusers are kept within the "worst of the worst" group, to continue to be shamed through the registry with it's related isolation based laws, than the ultimate outcome will not be less offending, but what is now happening more and more, LESS REPORTING!

And one final note, in these days of feminine superiority through the court systems here in the US, these laws will often be used as false allegations by mothers who wish a divorce and also want the courts to hand them the majority of the family assets and complete un-contested custody of the children. These accused men, are so often convicted only on the wife's allegations and then face not only the loss of house, job, and children, but are then lumped into this "worst of the worst" group. They are also looked at through the forced therapy system we have in place, as those who "are not willing to take responsibility for their crime", a crime they didn't even do. ■

Vicki Henry

A Woman at W.A.R.

Interview conducted by RSOA Magazine interviewer, Kate Logan assisted by Randy English

What would make a woman, a wife and mother begin to advocate for Sex Offenders? RSO Advocacy Magazine asked Vicki Henry, Director of W.A.R. (Women Against Registry) that very question. The answer was more complex than you may think. When talking with Vicki you understand very quickly that she is a passionate person, but not driven by emotion. Vicki is intelligent and she understands the subject of sex offender issues far better than most people. Please join us as we hear, in her own words, what makes a person advocate for the most hated people in the world today.

Kate begins the interview. Vicki, what brought you to the fight for sex offender law reform? "My son was in the military when a couple of the guys in his unit saw child pornography on his laptop and told their officer. My son confirmed it when asked and said he felt he had a problem with it and needed help. The officer said, 'Get the 'F-'out of here and don't do it anymore. We'll get you some help when you get back in the states.'

"It was maybe a day before leaving to return to the states that he was TDA (loaned out) to another unit, still in the same state but about 2 hours from the base where the counseling was available. Several months later he was transferred back to his original base. A little while after that he was taken into custody and arraigned for possession of child pornography. He sat in the

brig for 357 days before his court martial. He took a plea deal for 48 months with sex offender treatment at a facility which is supposedly the best place in the military; and they had so many folks fall into the sex offender status within the military that they had to add on to their facility. That is what brought me to this place. Some people say it didn't happen or whatever, well in our case it did."

In talking with Vicki we learned that her son wanted treatment but as far as society is concerned, those who want treatment can't just ask for it without punishment or reprimand. Vicki said, "If a person tells someone 'I have a problem with looking at child pornography' that person is, by law, obligated to report it and you have to be prosecuted before you can get help." The irony of this is that a person can admit to being addicted to drugs and receive help without being criminalized first! Vicki went on to say that a General came to see her son at the brig and wanted to talk to him. She told her son to tell the General that he would need to talk to the private attorney. The General stated he was afraid he was going to say that and he wanted to talk to her son about the "cover-up", because the whole unit was being investigated. They considered it a "cover-up" by those that knew. She said, 'Imagine that…the military accusing an individual of covering something up!' Vicki again stated, "That is what brought our family to

the fight."

When we asked Vicki how she felt when she found out her son was involved in child pornography, she responded by saying, "If people would be honest a lot of times there was some kind of indicator and maybe something they missed which is what kind of happened in our case. So I was surprised, but not totally surprised, because he was kind of protective of his laptop, and then when you think back, there was a couple of things that were cries for help which I should have paid attention to, and I think if more people were honest, they would say that."

Kate - How did you feel when you found out? "It literally brought me to my knees. I can't even say devastation is a good word. It just turned my world literally upside down. I had been a single mom for 15 years, raised my boys and they were raised in church, they didn't have the A+ grade thing going on but they made decent grades and were good kids. It was kind of hard to even imagine what was going on."

As the conversation went on, Vicki told us that her son had been sexually abused by his biological father years ago. This was determined when he was examined by the forensic psychologist who was hired by his private attorney. The psychologist report revealed that he was not a threat to society; he was not interested in kids and was looking for normal heterosexual

relationships. He had started looking at child pornography because he was trying to figure out why it happened to him since he was unable to reveal this to his mother.

We asked Vicki how she, as a mother, dealt with the news that her son was involved in child pornography? Her response was, "It's a grieving process. It's a feeling of supreme loss and a feeling of ultimate failure." Vicki went on to say that she supported her son. He worked hard and pushed others so they would make it through basic training. After achieving his goal that he wanted so badly, it was all stripped away after serving for three years. He was prosecuted, court martialed, stripped of pay, rank and lost his health and educational benefits while receiving a dishonorable discharge.

We asked Vicki what could be done to correct a system that has obviously failed her son and so many other military families? She replied, "The military system could have, at the point that they determined he had a problem, sent him back to the states and started him in some kind of treatment, BUT, the law says, of course, that they can't do that; they can't put them in treatment and put them in any group therapy situations until they have been adjudicated, and I think that is wrong. This is one of the reasons wives and mothers and whomever do not report these things; because they know what is going to happen and how life is going to be from that day forward." Vicki went on to say that psychiatrists and psychologists say that families who are reunited are better functioning than one that they keep away from everyone.

When we asked Vicki at what point she learned about the registry, she jokingly replied, "I was just like everyone else, I was a media educated person who was taught that everyone on the registry were monsters. I didn't realize until about 6 months after our family started this journey that he would be on the registry, but I had already figured out by reading and researching that it was going to probably happen."

Vicki revealed a startling situation within the system when she said, "My son had his first lie detector test 3 months after returning home on parole. He filled out a pre-test questionnaire and that is where they get the entrapment. He passed the lie detector test on a Monday. On Wednesday morning his parole officer called and said she would be by to do a visit later that day which was odd because they usually don't announce they are coming by. My son waited around and was even outside hitting golf balls in the front yard when they arrived. I had just arrived home from work when she and another officer came to our home for a visit. She did a walk through, checked the gun safe to make sure it was locked and we stood and talked. Two days later at 7:15 a.m. the PO knocked on the door and my husband answers the door and lets her and her associate inside. I came into the living room and she asked if my son was there? I said he was asleep and she asked if I could get him. When he came into the kitchen she asked if he remembered the stipulations of his parole and he acknowledged. She then said he had violated them and the deputy came up behind him and handcuffed him. She then advised on her walkie that he was in custody and about 22 law enforcement came into the house. They forced me and my husband to sit on the couch while they 'paraded' all through the house; searched my son's room and bathroom." Vicki stated there were, "U.S. Marshals, county and Parole Office people they were parked out down the road and around the corner and scared the (H--) out of the neighbors. My son asked one U.S. Marshal, 'Why are there so many of you here?' He replied, 'Oh, because we didn't have anything else to do today.' My son became so overwhelmed that he passed out and dropped to the floor. They brought a nurse (with a side arm) in to check him out and waived off the ambulance stating he was OK. The PO took my son's cell phone, my computer CPU, a camcorder (with no batteries) he had gotten while deployed and two "girlie" magazines. One of the officers asked if we knew he had the magazines because he was not supposed to have any adult magazines while he is on parole. My son later advised me that he bought those magazines at the brig and if they had looked in the lower right corner they would have seen his name and squad bay. They took him to the county jail and then a few days later the military picked him up and took him back to the brig for a violation hearing. The charges stated he was on Facebook. It was not his Facebook account; it was mine" (Vicki's) but the monitoring system they had placed on our computer as a condition of keeping it in the house could not differentiate as to who of the three people using the computer went where on it.

"There was a preliminary hearing where I testified by phone. The recommendation sent to Washington was that my son should be sent back out on parole but, the folks in Washington wanted to wait for the final analysis on my computer. So my son spent 3 months at the brig until everything was finalized. The final report stated there was no child pornography found on the computer. The parole officer put 37 stipulations on him so our private attorney said he needed to just stay there and finish the last 8 months because the P.O. would make his life miserable" Vicki said, "After they left with him that day, I was so devastated. I spent the rest of the day in the recliner, staring at the carpet on the floor stating "I don't want to live anymore."

We asked Vicki how this

has affected her son's life. She responded by saying that, "While on parole he had applied to different places here and there and got so frustrated he picked up the yellow pages and just started calling businesses. He finally got a job with a lawn care company. He worked for about 2 months before they came and arrested him again. As far as how this affected his relationships, the first girl he dated, he had to list her address on the registry as an alternate address because he would stay there several days during a 30 day period. When he got back home he again applied many places and could not even get hired at Wal-Mart because of the background check. He currently has a job and enjoys the work. The registry has affected his life to the point that he carries a flashlight and a pocketknife with him for protection as he is not allowed to have any other type of protection."

As we continued talking with Vicki, we asked her if she feared for her son's life because of the registry and increased vigilantism of those listed on the public registry. She told us, "I do fear for his life and have taken all the steps allowed to protect him while at our residence or with me." She used an example of how he stopped to help some puppies along the road and she told him not to stop anymore, "especially if someone is following you." She also commented that there were some people living in their subdivision who are not thrilled with him living there. When we asked how long her son would be on the registry she said, "For life, unless we get it changed."

As we continued talking with Vicki, we inquired how she got into this fight; was it gradual or did she jump right in? Vicki replied, "I found a group called Daily Strength – Families of Sex Offenders and through them found the RSOL organization. Shortly after that I signed on with their Minute Men group. I am hard headed and

don't take no for an answer. I am not intimidated and therefore a challenge to people. My husband would say, 'The laws are the laws,' and I would tell him that doesn't mean they can't be changed. I am hardworking and have learned the true meaning of civil and human rights activism."

Vicki is also a leader in W.A.R., Women Against Registry. She told us that when she first started the fight, "it was for my son and what could do to help him, but now it is for everybody on the registry." Vicki went on to say, "Everyone deserves a second chance, even those in civil commitment who will never get the chance unless these laws change."

We asked her if there is anyone she would exclude in her advocacy and she replied, "The ones I would exclude are the ones that say, if you let me out I will do it again." She went on to say that those who work hard to change their lives deserve a chance, "Your past shouldn't determine or define your future."

Vicki, we hear some in the movement say things like Romeos or streakers are not like rapists or those with child victims. What reaction do you have to comments like that? "Well, they're not. Each person and each case is different and they should be judged accordingly. To me it would be wrong to say they are all the same, but they ALL do deserve the same second chance if they are willing to work to make the needed changes.

We feel the same way, but do you see comments like these as counterproductive to the movement as a whole? "Yes. I think they are, if you name a lot of different scenarios that's one thing, but if you just advocate for one thing like Romeos or child pornography cases, I don't like that. I don't have time to spend on one issue. We have to advocate for all the issues.

"I see our movement as needing to present legislators with the problem that the registry is causing

to families of registrants. And I'm from the old school, 'don't just bring me a problem, bring me a solution too.' So we need solutions. And I think that our solution is to educate legislators. Just like we did in our state. When we started talking with legislators, they didn't have a clue of what studies had said or anything. They didn't have a clue of the impact that these laws were having on families of registrants. So I think reaching state legislators is the start. Then advocating for programs that would teach parents how to truly protect their children, I think that is the key, stopping the problem before it becomes a problem."

Vicki, if you had a magic wand, what would you do with the registry? Vicki laughed, "There wouldn't be a public registry. There would be a minimal registry for law enforcement only. Risk assessment is a key, it's important. But I think that streaker and some others may not even need risk assessment. Then, after that, help registrants get on with their lives so they can move forward by providing them the support to keep offense free and get jobs and homes to live in."

That would be a positive step forward. Next, what are your views on the Second Chance Act excluding sex offenses? "I spoke with a woman in the SMART office and according to her and another person I spoke with, they're not excluded, on paper anyway, but when it trickles down, when it gets down to who gets a second chance, that's what is going to happen."

As we ended the interview Vicki made one last comment, "I think we're starting to see things turn around with registry laws, but it's still going to be a long haul."

We have to agree with Vicki on all of the points she made. We are proud to be working in this movement with such a devoted advocate for change.■

THE SEX OFFENDER ERA; a PROPAGANDA WAR

by Al Lynne

The Sex Offender Era covers a period of about twenty years and it is no more than a journey of myth and fantasy.

What began as a small voice in a town of tragedy, reverberated into a majestic colossal of expensive, unreasonable and ineffective laws and legislation. By naming laws after victims of heinous murders to compel an audience weeping over the pain to demand justice were no match for the sound squelched scientific evidence from the professionals who recognized the wolf in sheep's skin. No politician would even dare oppose the peoples passion while that name remained grafted onto that parchment.

It was a brilliant propaganda tactic. Who would oppose it if it were named after the victim of the crime? The tactic worked so well, it was tried again and again with unprecedented success. However it's success continues to feed the minds of the simple and naive trampling over any opportunity of sound reliable evidence to the contrary.

It is a Propaganda War and the scope is centered on an easy target. Sex Offenders are not at the top of everyone's Favorite's List. More so the propaganda tactics continued as news articles used words like "Pedophiles" and Predators" because as it makes for great sensationalized stories and feeds the hungry simple minded which were starving for justice and retribution, it also condemned anyone which had this label pasted on to them.

Propaganda is defined as information, ideas, or rumors deliberately spread widely to help or harm a person, group, movement, institution, nation, etc. Propaganda was used quite often, from ancient history even to the present day and is an effective tool to draw popularity to a given subject. One interesting example from ancient history is the Great Fire of Rome that burned for nearly a week and Nero blamed it on the Christians because they were an unpopular class of people and an easy target for the propaganda. This marked the beginning of early Christian Persecution which was listed outside of the Bible. Another example would be during early America of what is famously known as the Boston Massacre. Each side conflicted in their stories, however, propaganda from the event stirred up patriotism in many Americans.

Hitler relied heavily on propaganda and even had a division called *"Ministry of*

Propaganda". Had it not been for Hitlers Propaganda tactics, there most likely would not have been a World War two. If we were to dig deeper into the mind of Adolph Hitler regarding Propaganda, it has a startling similarity with the development of the Sex Offender era.

"...The art of propaganda consists precisely in being able to awaken the imagination of the public through an appeal to their feelings ..."

"...The great majority of a nation is so feminine in its character and outlook that its thought and conduct are ruled by sentiment rather than by sober reasoning..."

"...Propaganda must not investigate the truth objectively and, in so far as it is favourable to the other side, present it according to the theoretical rules of justice; yet it must present only that aspect of the truth which is favourable to its own side..."

"... The receptive powers of the masses are very restricted, and their understanding is feeble. On the other hand, they quickly forget. Such being the case, effective propaganda must be confined to a few bare essentials and those must be expressed as far as possible in stereotyped formulas. These slogans should be persistently repeated until the very last individual has come to grasp the idea that has been put forward..."

- excerpts from Mein Kampf chapter 6 English Version.

There is no doubt that by using a child's abduction, sexual assault or murder and pasting it onto legislation would appeal to peoples feelings. No politician in their right mind would dare oppose it for it would no doubt lead to political suicide because as far as the people are concerned, that legislation was authored in the name of that child and by opposing it would also be opposing the justice due to that child. It was primarily the attitude of the people rather than sound thinking when it came to Legislation with a Child's name attached to it. The contents of the legislation was not of primary concern more than the peoples sentiment for all the people knew was that this legislation would pacify the passion for justice of that child whose name entitles the legislation. It also needed to move very quickly because had anyone researched the details it might have failed. Thus the truth was not investigated objectively.

From the time the Sex Offender era began with the tragedy of Jacob Wetterling, nearly to the present day, all arguments were one sided. There was very little opposition and so it was easy to slide legislation through.

Also as these types of Child Labeled Legislation appeared, so did slogans and sayings which were easy to believe and easy to sell. Things like "... Sex Offenders can't be cured...", "... Sex Offenders have a high risk of re-offending..." and "...A typical Sex Offender will molest 117 children..." They appeared constantly and daily most times. News media would use words like "...Pedophiles..." and say Pedophiles are loose in your neighborhood or Pedophiles may be living next door to you, so that eventually the word "Pedophiles" became interchangeable with "Sex Offenders"; and not only in a slogan like manner, but also intensely appealing to the peoples feelings and opinions rather than sober reasoning.

In almost amazing similarity, the Sex Offender era developed with the exact same principles that Hitler used to fool an entire nation. Now, even when there is sound reasoning, expert testimony and accurate reliable statistics, they are apathetically ignored because of the efficacy of this propaganda tactic in which repeated slogans or sayings sunk deep into the minds of the simple and permeated our society.

Once the Propaganda succeeds in winning the hearts of the people, it becomes most difficult to reverse.

Politically is the most difficult because the standard response is always "... they are coddling sex offenders...", and would be political suicide for any politician which would appear to side with Sex Offenders.

News Media is the next most difficult because most of these companies and networks rely heavily on ratings.

If ratings are reduced, the value of sponsors are reduced. The third most difficult is the people. In every society, once an idea is promoted and has gained popularity among a greater majority, especially if it is done repeatedly, over a period of time, it becomes ingrained in the minds of the people, regardless whether the information is true to fact or not.

Take for example commercials which we see during our favorite programs. How many times have we seen a commercial repeat itself? Which one's do you remember? Which one's do you actually use because it was advertised? Believe it or not, Advertising is very similar to propaganda tactics. The more times an ad can be presented to the mind, the greater chances that it will be burned into the memory cells.■

Is there a solution?

There is a parable of an heir; an attorney was tasked to deliver a message to a man informing him of a prodigious inheritance from an unknown distant relative. During his travel to the heir, he was intercepted by townspeople and the townspeople rejected him because he was a leper. The

townspeople ejected him from the town and when the word came to the heir, he rejected him also and refused to speak with him; resulting in the loss of the inheritance. The attorney still to this day makes an attempt to deliver the inheritance to the man, and the man fervidly continues to reject him because of his leprosy.

This is how most of us in the field of activism feel, fighting against a monster of opposition, with an unpopular message, being considered vile by most; especially the Vigilantes, with solutions for nearly all of the problems with Child Sexual Abuse, Sex Offender Management, Protection and Security for families.

We are the very few who have actually investigated the reliable, facts and truths objectively without the influence of sentiment or feeble passion. We are not ignorant of the propaganda tactics and wise to the Political wrangling and News Media ratings whores. However our message is only a small voice in a deep canyon surrounded by doubt, suspicion, disfavor and rejection. But we continue to keep fighting, not primarily against opponents of Child Sexual Abuse, but for that which is right, for that which bares reasoning for freedom and justice, for that which every living person is entitled to which is what our constitution is supposed to protect us with and that is our right to life, liberty and the pursuit of happiness. ∎

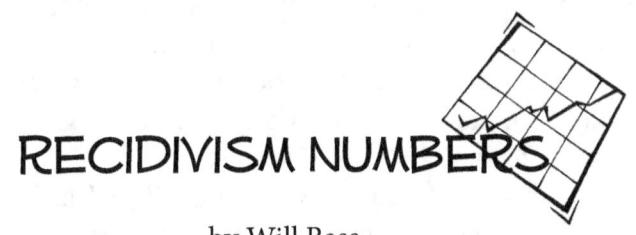

RECIDIVISM NUMBERS

by Will Bass

One thing must be pointed out at this time, all of these studies work with recently released prisoners during the transition time from prison life to reintegration into society. In order to get an accurate set of re-offense numbers for the general population of sex offenders. A study must take into effect all of the people that have been out for long periods of time and have not re-offend example, the total number of people on the registry and the number of those people that re-offend. Many people firmly believe that all sex offenders are violent psychopaths who are incurable, and will continually re-offend as long as they are out of jail. That is why they believe all sex offenders have to be taken off the streets forever, and closely monitored for life, and prevented from ever living anywhere near children—their own or others. Surprisingly, the data collected by State and Federal agencies do not support this myth. In fact, the majority of sex offenders do not go on to re-offend. That is borne out by a number of reports cited below.

Department of Justice's own report states that the recidivism rate of released sex offenders is only 3.5% In their report entitled *"Recidivism of Sex Offenders Released from Prison in 1994,"* it states, *"Within the first 3 years following their release from prison in 1994, 3.5% (339 of the 9,691) were reconvicted for a sex crime within the 3-year follow-up period."* 1% per year Source: US Dep't of Justice, *"Recidivism of Sex Offenders Released from Prison in 1994."* pg-24 Published 11/2003.

In this study, there were 27 times more non-sex offender ex-convicts than there were released sex-offenders. The ex-convicts who were not sex offenders actually committed six times more new sex crimes than did the released sex offenders. This study showed that 87% of new sex crimes were committed by ex-convicts, not by registered sex offenders (USDOJ 2003.) This study looked at only individuals who have a prior criminal record. When

one considers that most sex offenses are committed by those who have no prior criminal record, it is easy to see that the vast majority of new sex crimes are committed by someone other than a registered sex offender. (USDOJ 1994)

This is not a mistake or a statistical artifact. Other studies show similar trends, with recidivism rates for released convicted sex offenders of from 2.5 to 11 percent. Time periods in the studies ranges from 3 to 15 years. In United States v. Mound, 157 F.3d 1153, 1154, (8th Cir. 1998) (en banc), four dissenting Judges cite Law Review articles citing statistics finding the recidivism rate of released sex offenders is the second lowest rate of recidivism of all convicted felons. In State v. Krueger, Case No. 76624 (December 19, 2000, Eighth Judicial District of Ohio, unreported), two female Judges reversed a Sexual Predator adjudication, finding the statute is based on a false assumption and in essence, an "old wives tale" of popular beliefs contradicted by empirical data.

By writing the National Criminal Justice Reference Center, P.O. Box 6000, Rockville, Maryland 20849-6000, you can obtain the following reports.

NCJ-163392 (February 7, 1997), Sex Offenses and Offenders: An Analysis of Data on Rape and Sexual Assault, finds the recidivism rate of 2,214 convicted rapists released from prison was 7.7% after three years. The only category of crimes with a lower recidivism rate are those persons convicted of murder (6.8%).

NCJ-193427 (June, 2002), Recidivism of Prisoners Released in 1994, finds the recidivism rate of 3,138 convicted rapists released from prison was 2.5% after three years. 8/10 of 1% per year The only category of crimes with a lower recidivism rate are those persons convicted of murder (1.2%). In April, 2001, the Ohio Department of Rehabilitation and Correction (ODRC) released a report also on the recidivism rate of released sex offenders. In Ten-Year Recidivism Follow-Up of 1989 Sex Offender Releases, Office of Policy, Bureau of Planning and Evaluation, Paul Konicek, Principle Researcher, (available at www.drc.state.oh.us), the recidivism rate of 879 sex offenders released from Ohio's prisons in 1989, after ten (10) years, was found to be 8% for new sex offenses.

The ODRC study finds its results as typical, citing to:

1) Gibbons, Soothill, and Way, found in Furby, Weinrott & Blackshaw, 1989. (Twelve year study finding sex offender recidivism rate of 4%) 3/10 of 1% per year.

2) jacks study, found in Furby, Weinrott & Blackshaw, 1989. (fifteen year study of 3424 offenders found sex offenders recidivism rate of 3.7%) 2/10 of 1% per year.

3) New York Department of Corrections, nine year follow-up study. Finding a 6% rate of recidivism for new sex offenses. 6/10 of 1% per year.

These studies are cited on page 11 of the ODRC report. At page 15 of the report, the overall findings are summarized. The ODRC finds, "Contrary to the popular idea that sex offenders are repeatedly returning to prison for further sex crimes, in this population a sex offender recidivating for a new sex offense within 10 years of release was a relatively rare occurrence." Id. at page 15, 4. (Love 2002)13

The widely recognized researcher on psychological evaluation Robyn M. Dawes in his book House of Cards *"Psychology and Psychotherapy Built on Myth"*, stated *"A person who claims that a treatment is effective must demonstrate that it has an effect in comparison to a hypothetical counterfactual, obtained through construction of a randomly constituted control group."* Such randomized experiments are very necessary in evaluating treatments for emotional disorders and one of the best is what is called a "Wait List Control". This was used in the Florida Department of Health and Rehabilitative study from 1984 the people who had completed treatment re-offended in a sex crime at 13.6% and other crimes at 18.6%. Those who did not complete treatment at 6.5% for sex offense and 12.9% for other crimes and those that were on the list, but did not get into treatment re-offended in sex crimes at 5% and other crimes at 0%. The more the treatment, the more the criminal activity!

Most studies nationally reported rates ranging from 27.6% to 41.0% for subsequent offense." They did not point out that those numbers are only

for persons in treatment. The *Jacks Study* in 1962 looked into non-treated offenders showed the re-offense rate of 3.7% over 15 years that's 2/10 of 1% per year, this must be used as the base line set as laid out by Robyn Dawes any treatment program with a re-offence rate higher then 3.7% for a 15 year period must be considered a failure of the program not the individuals in it. ■

What's missing from this page?

Your ad!

contact us today! postmaster@rso-advocacy.org

Vigilantism

by Randy English

Part one

It is an age old problem. People become angry; they feel the government is not doing their job, so they take action. It's called vigilante justice. Vigilante justice... if that isn't a contradiction I don't know what is.

Vigilantism and the public registry

The recent murders of two registered citizens in Washington State have yet again brought this subject before the nation. Much like the 2006 murders of two registrants in the state of Maine, these latest murders have a link to the public registry. Some may say that this is to be expected and well worth the cost to protect children. They may also feel that it is rare, but is it?

Taking the year 2009 as an example we will find that murders of registered citizens is not uncommon. Let's look at just a few of the murdered registered citizens from that year:

Registered citizen, Qaddafi Nick, 35-years-old of Riverside, California. **Murdered**. *"During his blood test, defendant commented he had to 'take care of a rapist.' At his arraignment on March 9, 2009, defendant bragged he had 'popped' the victim 'in the chest three times' for 'molesting."*

Registered citizen, Dale Ellis, 20-years-old of Texas. **Murdered**. *"The pair knew each other, and it was well known in the homeless community that Grammer disliked Ellis for being a registered sex offender."*

Registered citizen, Scott Dana Malmstrom, 47-years-old of California. **Murdered**. *"A white supremacist gang member testified that Cole bragged in jail about killing a child molester."*

Registered citizen John Stouffer, 25-year-old of Ohio. **Murdered**. *"was found stabbed to death in his room... because Stouffer was a convicted sex offender."*

Registered citizen, William Ballance, 47-years-old of Ohio. **Murdered**. *"Suspect, Hartsell had lived with Ballance, a convicted sex offender, until about a week ago."*

This is but a portion of the murders of registrants during the year of 2009. Since 2003 the number of registrants being murdered has risen sharply. Many times those responsible for these murders are never found, all that are left are the headlines detailing the crimes.

What about 2012?

Surely by 2012 the public has become accustomed to the sex offender registry. Surely vigilantism has decreased.

Not at all, let's have a brief look:

"Body found in cemetery identified as sex offender. Michigan. Murdered."

Registered citizen Donald Olynn Cook, Virginia. Murdered "Daughter fears sex offender's killing was a case of vigilante justice".

Registered citizen, Bobby Ray Buck 33-year-old of North Carolina, Murdered "Man found shot to death in a car. he's a registered sex offender according to the state's registry."

Registered citizens Jerry Wayne Ray, 56, and Gary Lee Blanton, 28, of PORT ANGELES, Washington, Murdered. "Suspect Drum had a "particular animus toward sex offenders.""

And once again the list goes on and on and it is escalating.

Some people with a vigilante attitude are calling murderers like Drum, a hero. We have to ask, "is this mind-set considered sane?" It certainly is cruel, especially when these vigilantes call, harass and post sick comments on the facebook page of the wife of one of the slain men.

In this part of the Vigilante series we have discussed murders, however, murder of registered citizens is not the only effect vigilantes are having.

From beating, to vandalism to online threats, vigilantes are targeting registered citizens in a very deliberate way, so deliberate that they set up websites for the purpose of online stalking and harassment of registrants, their families and friends. Some of these criminals brag about their actions online and in letters to the press. In the end though they are nothing more than thugs; bullies hiding behind a computer monitor.

In future articles we will unmake the vigilantes, exposing them for their criminal acts that they claim are all in the name of being upright, concerned citizens. ◼

Reflections of History

by Randy English - 2010

There stands no greater threat to humanity than a ruler who fails to learn from the past. The mistakes and misdeeds of men and monsters have been preserved in literature and in recorded history. Young men and women spend years in school learning about atrocities committed by men with names like Hitler and Goering. Some of these go on to college where they learn even more and yet for some reason once they leave these schools of learning this knowledge fades away. In time some of these people run for political office and once elected they begin to push for laws to control those who elected them. It is an age old problem one that has brought about such sayings as, "absolute power corrupts absolutely."

A history lesson is in order for some of these elected officials regarding sex offenders.

Germany May 15, 1871 - First Version of Paragraph 175 - Unnatural fornication, whether between persons of the male sex or of humans with beasts, is to be punished by imprisonment; a sentence of loss of civil rights may also be passed.

In 1935, the Nazis broadened the law so that the courts could pursue any "lewd act" whatsoever, even one involving no physical contact, such as masturbating next to each other, leading to the possibility of punishment for acts as mild as kissing, fondling, or mutual masturbation that previously would not have been considered criminal. This was not merely an aberration of the Nazi era: the courts in the Federal Republic (West Germany) understood the term similarly. Convictions multiplied by a factor of ten to about 8,000 per year. Furthermore, the Gestapo could transport suspected offenders to concentration camps without any legal justification at all (even if they had been acquitted or already served their sentence in jail). Thus, between 5,000 and 15,000 sex offenders were forced into concentration camps, where they were identified by the pink triangle. The majority of them died there.

According to the official rationale, Paragraph 175 was amended in the interest of the moral health of the *Volk* – the German people

This aggravation of the severity of Paragraph 175 in 1935 increased the number of convictions tenfold, to 8,000 annually. Only about half of the prosecutions resulted from police work; about 40 percent resulted from private accusations (*Strafanzeige*) by non-participating observers, and about 10 percent were denouncements by employers and institutions.

In contradistinction to normal police, the Gestapo were authorized to take sex offenders into preventive detention (*Schutzhaft*) of arbitrary duration without an accusation (or even after an acquittal). This was often the fate of so-called "repeat offenders": at the end of their sentences, they were not freed but sent for additional "reeducation" (*Umerziehung*) in a concentration camp. Only about 40 percent of these pink triangle prisoners – whose numbers amounted to an estimated 10,000 – survived the camps. Some of them, after their release by the Allied Forces, were placed back in prison, because they had not yet finished court-mandated terms of imprisonment for sexual acts.

A Pattern Returns

Once again sex offenders are the target of political leaders. Through a myriad of laws one stacked on the back of another a large drag net is being cast in the United States. Predictions were made several years past that sex offender laws would incur greater penalties and the outcome would be death camps. Does this hypothesis have any basis in fact? Here are some examples.

"Cantwell Legislation to Create Nationwide Sex Offender Database, to Enact Stricter Registration Standards and Penalties."

"WASHINGTON — A bill passed by the Senate that stiffens registration laws against sexual predators contained legislation by U.S. Rep. Mark Foley and U.S. Sen. Bill Nelson."

"Jane Velez-Mitchell says tougher penalties are needed to keep sex offenders from committing more crimes."

"Senator Dan Newberry wants to put all Level II and III sex offenders on "Electronic Monitoring for life.""

"House Bill 2965, proposed by Rex Duncan, would expand the penalties for sex offenders, allowing repeat offenders to face life in prison without parole or the death penalty."

"Maryland lawmakers are poised to get tougher on sex offenders, with bills already being proposed to expand registry information, establish lifetime supervision and require involuntary confinement in state mental institutions after a jail sentence."

Hitler would be proud.

Once Hitler found success in setting up national registries, he expanded them. This expansion was gradual. This gave the public time to adjust. By the time the Jews were being murdered in the concentrations camps the German people had been lulled into believing everything Hitler told them about the monsters he was locking away and killing. What started with the most hated of society expanded to include anyone the German government did not like. Could this happen in the United States? It is not likely unless the government begins to set up other registries.

JOHNSON CITY — Tennessee needs a "Repeat DUI Offender" registry similar to the state sex offender registry people can check out on the Internet, state Sen. Mike Faulk says.

Renewed Push for National Arson Registry - Democratic Sens. Barbara Boxer and Dianne Feinstein introduced legislation Thursday that would establish the registry. It complements a similar bill backed by Reps. Mary Bono Mack, a Republican, and Adam Schiff, a Democrat, which has been in a House Judiciary subcommittee since March.

State's Now Sprouting Drug Offender Registry - **Internet registries of rapists or pedophiles are available in every state, but a new breed** **of criminal now is experiencing the notoriety of being "outed" online—people convicted of making or selling methamphetamine.**

Hawaii is now considering a murderer's registry, much like a sex offender registry, after two paroled murderers committed more crimes. http://apublicdefender.com/2007/08/07/now-a-murderers-registry-is-there-a-better-solution/

Just a Matter of Time

All of the elements are once again in place. More than likely the execution chambers have already been built and many lawmakers are eager to take their place in history alongside the greats like Adolph Hitler. No matter how they push these laws, whether through the tough on crime line or the tough on pedophiles cry, the outcome is the same, mass murder being smiled upon by the government. Today history is once again being made and just as in the 1930's, people are speaking out about the atrocities looming on the horizon. But these pleas for sanity are falling on the deaf ears of men and woman many of which have the same mentality as Hitler. The question is, will these blood thirsty politicians be there to flip the switch in the gas chambers or will they have others do their dirty work for them? One last reflection for today's politicians to ponder. What was it that stopped Hitler's madness? It was called World War II. Our future is not set in stone. There is still time to call political leaders back to their senses. If you do not, you will be as guilty as they will be, on the day the executions begin.∎

"What experience and history teach is this - that people and governments never have learned anything from history, or acted on principles deduced from it."

G. W. F. Hegel

Follow Up to "Reflection of History"

2012

by Randy English

After I wrote the original article for SOSEN, I was bashed by many including some in the reform movement. They pointed out that it is not good to talk about Nazi Germany in comparison with current sex offender laws.

So my question is, why not? If you actually read the whole article you will see the comparisons. The laws in Germany started out against sex offenders and in time were broadened to encompass many others. We are seeing that today here in the United States. The Registry itself has become so broad that it is ineffective for its original intent.

The original article was written in 2010, so what has changed in that time? Well first off, the State of Ohio enacted the far reaching AWA. Then the Ohio Supreme Court struck down many of its provisions on several grounds, from being punitive to being retroactive. Other states have opted out of this overreaching law and still others have embraced it.

Like Germany, the United States has set up programs that keep some sex offenders detained indefinitely after their criminal sentences are completed. These laws have been deemed constitutional by the courts, just as they were in Germany in the 1940's.

What else is new? Many things and we will start with the top dog in the law enforcement group. (http://www.interstatecompact.org/LinkClick.aspx?fileticket=ao9ap27EWE4%3D&tabid=358&mid=3148)

If you go to the link above you will find that the U.S. Marshals Service is now requiring that all sex offenders, registered or not, to apply to them before traveling to a foreign county. This law was passed supposedly because of sex tourism. However registered sex offenders are not sex tourists. The arrest record for the past ten years proves this out.

The next thing that Congress is poised to do is to grant the Marshals Service the right to write their own search warrants, without the need of a judge. This is unprecedented in U.S. history. This expansion of power should frighten all U.S. citizens. I expect it has since more U.S. citizens are now leaving the U.S. than in any other time in the history of this country. How will the courts react to this overreaching of Congress? Time will tell but if the courts remain silent, congress is likely to write them right out of the picture.

In other news, sex offenders are being cast out of social networking, while at the same time government and the business sector are embracing sites such as Facebook. Just a few minutes of web surfing and you will find that if you do not have a Facebook account, you are left out of the conversation in most news stories, especially the political ones.

This ostracizing of sex offenders is no less repugnant than what was done to sex offenders in Nazi Germany. History is repeating itself and one day people will look back and list names like Bobby Jindal, not as a hero but as a misinformed, angry person bent on ridding his little corner the world of sex offenders.

During the past two years new studies have emerged that have conclusively proven that sex offenders do not pose the threat that legislators were led to believe. We have also learned that sex offenders are a money tree for gps providers, lie detector providers, government sponsored programs, civil commitment facilities and even some families of victims.

State approved treatment providers are also cashing in on the trend. But the big winners seem to be the up-start web-sites that play on the fear of parents.

HomeFacts and Offendex are but two of these for-profit web-sites that claim to be all about protection of children. But they are not. These sites do not have accurate information and OfffendeX will remove the names of registrants for a fee. It's all about the money.

The more you look at the current registry scheme the more you will find that it is not about public safety. It has however become an effective tool for limiting your freedoms. Did I say your freedoms? Yes, because whether you are a registered offender or not, your freedoms have been eroded due to the registry. You see, every time legislators say they are talking away a freedom against a registrant and you are so excited, well guess what, you lose too. Those freedoms that are taken away from registrants are fought for in court and once the court approves that loss, it forms what is called "case law." That means that if the government one day wants to strip you of those same freedoms, they can do it, because the court has already given them a nod to do so. This is what happened in Germany between 1871 and 1940.

Will you learn from the past, or will you once again say that I should talk about Nazi Germany. It doesn't really matter though, because either way, you and I are caught up in a repeat of history■

The duty of a patriot is to protect his country from its government.

Thomas Paine

Do you have something to say?

Do you have a story to tell?

Do you have a news item you want us to cover?

Do you need someone to listen?

Do you want to join the fight but don't know what to do?

Do you fear because of vigilantes?

Are you the parent or friend of an RSO who is seeking information?

Are you alone and isolated because of residency laws?

Are you in prison and seeking information on laws and court cases?

Are you to afraid to get involved in the fight but know you should?

Contact us! We are RSO Advocacy.
We are a strong voice. We have resources.

postmaster@rso-advocacy.org

Brace For Impact

by Al Lynne

"Brace For Impact" was the title of a Blog thread as I began my daily routine of reading forums and news. It was another Abduction/Sexual Assault/Murder of a child. I should have been more sympathetic toward the parents of this poor child, but my selfish thoughts were focused on whether I should prepare for another tsunami of Sex Offender Legislation.

This was about a week before the discovery of Terry Black. I set up daily alerts for Sierra Newbold, the victim of this heinous crime. I cringed as each day passed, white knuckled because if it turned out to be a registered sex offender, then look out, here we go again.

I was really upset at the journalists handling the story, too much information was left out and of course, the police were not releasing any information.

It was a sloppy crime, so I expected evidence to be easily discovered. They said there was no evidence of a break in, but, were the doors and windows left unlocked? Were there any footprints or fingerprints? Did anyone hear any screaming or scuffling? Did she just wander off outside by herself? What about her siblings or other neighborhood kids? Other questions like these were going through my head and it just made me frustrated that none of the journalists were even posing any of them.

Each day it was "Police are still not releasing information," and I was thinking, "Gee the Barney Fife crew." It could not be that difficult, as sloppy as this crime was, there had to be an obvious trail of evidence leading to the perpetrator.

Day after day, still no news. It was getting frustrating. The Barney Fife crew did release a notice not to panic, and I thought, hah, don't panic, yeah, right, a precious little girl just got abducted, sexually assaulted and murdered and that's the best you can do?

Already I'm thinking, "... Sierra's Law ..." and what kind of useless legislation are the Pandering Politicians going to wave in our face this time? What kind of headlines are we going to read? " ... Child Abducted, Sexually Assaulted and Murdered by another Repeat Pedophile Scumbag..." And oh, I can just hear the public saying, "Kill them all," "Cut off their protruding members," and "Why do we let them out of prison in the first place?" I know the routine; I've heard it time and time again. It's like a broken record. Oh my gosh, and I can just imagine the vigilante's; they'll have a hay day and a free ride with the public's approval.

During this intense week for me, anticipating some type of decent news from our ratings whores, most of the news regarding Sierra was buried under Political News, which dominated most of our major networks.

After about three or four days, I began to wonder why there was no news that the local "Sex Offenders" were not interviewed (cough-- harassed). We hear it every time there is a child abduction. "All of the Local Sex Offenders Were Checked Out," and every time it produces absolutely no results in their case. Just maybe the public is getting tired of hearing the same old rhetoric, but that's just my own wishful thinking.

After about a week of heightened anxiety, it finally hit the news that the perpetrator was apprehended. It is a wonder that Terry Black didn't just accidentally stumble into the police department and trip into a jail cell. The way the events went down, it was almost as if he wanted to get arrested. He walks into a bank and robs it for $100, gets confronted by some local women who recognizes the stolen vehicle he was about to use, walks in a store to get change for the $100 bill, and walks back in to change one of the twenty dollar bill's. It was said that he didn't seem "all there" as if he was in a daze.

For someone who allegedly abducted, sexually assaulted and murdered a little child, it seems strange to me why he would even still be in town. Why didn't he make a get-away? Doesn't he realize that the authorities are looking for the perpetrator of a recently murdered child?

He is finally arrested and police are praised for such fine police work.

As the public's fury is evidenced in online news comments, you know the same old "...death penalty..." , "...torture...", "...put him in General Population, they'll

know what to do..." I am still left with unanswered questions like: Why did he do it? Why did he murder the poor child? Why did he target that particular person? Does he have a history of sexual abuse? Does he have a history of mental illness?

I've got to know because how could this have been prevented? How are we able to secure ourselves from this ever happening again? What are the signs that a person would manifest which would indicate this type of behavior is iminent?

According to most news reports, he did have a history of criminal behavior. None of which was sexually related. He did have a family and children, but no reports of abuse or child sexual abuse.

Where are all the politicians on this one? What law could you have possibly passed that would have prevented such a tragedy? Could it be that the harder you try, the worse it gets? Do you think that even harsher laws will prevent it from happening again? Well it's too late for this little child, she is dead and you didn't do a good enough job. Maybe you should pass laws that will test everyone ever arrested for Child Sexual Abuse. Maybe you should test everyone who has a Wife and Children who has a criminal history. Maybe you should test every male to be sure. Maybe you should put everyone on a registry, just in case because if it can save just one child, then it is worth it. It is your fault Mr. Politician for even considering that passing a law or that tightening restrictions on Sex Offenders would save this little child. Your arrogance and ignorance has caused more grief to the victims of Child Sexual Abuse. You said you would do what it takes to save

these children, well what did you do to save this child? What law did you pass that saved this child from being abducted? What restrictions did you approve that prevented this child from being sexually assaulted? What penalties have you pronounced that deterred a lunatic from murdering this child?

The law and the judicial system are limited only to one main specific fact, that no one has an argument for, and that is that the law can only become involved after a crime has been committed. You can pass a hundred laws, or even a thousand, and spend ten's of millions of Tax Dollar's and the fact still remains that the law is limited in the fact that it cannot prevent a crime from being committed.

However, prevention is the key, and the judicial system is useless when it comes to prevention.

We live in a world of dangers and hazards. It would be foolish to consider otherwise. We must learn to protect ourselves because the judicial system and law enforcement are limited in their abilities.

So as society continues to seek retribution and vengeance, I continue to contemplate and study on just how something like this can be prevented, how we can secure our children, how can we protect ourselves from such a horrible crime?

Now I'm not going to consider Terry Black guilty like most ratings whores, I still have respect for our Constitution. It was a sloppy crime and it amazed me that the investigation dragged out for so long. But if he did do this ungodly act, what was going through his mind? How can a person become so depraved without showing some signs? I want to know what

goes on in a mind like this so all of us can be prepared.

The greatest problem we have today is that Society has the habit of relying on the government. Government always seems to have a way of developing greater problems.

To the family of Sierra Newbold, my sympathies go out to them, and my condolences, because my heart is cut more so than most of the public because every time something like this occurs, the eyes of all society become fastened to those of us who are sentenced to register as sex offenders and we suffer the consequences of these heinous acts of which we had nothing to do with. It hurts even more so, and is a burden no one else will ever really understand unless or until they too are placed on the registry; and the direction in which are legislators are moving, don't be surprised if you too get stuck with this stigma. There are absolutely no signs from our legislators of it ever being improved, more so it appears to be becoming worse.

I am upset at ignorance. Society's ignorance and gullibility to propaganda. It is society's ignorance that causes the greater numbers of Child Sexual Abuse, and we all suffer the consequences because of it. I have done more good to reduce or eliminate Child Sexual Abuse than all of the Sex Offender laws and legislation ever has. For I am armed with the facts and science and because of that, I'm in a better position to educate people on how to prevent it. It is being educated with facts and the science which will win the battle against Child Sexual Abuse and apparently it is our politicians, by their own arrogance and ignorance who will be the enemy.■

SEPARATION OF POWERS UNDER THE UNITED STATES CONSTITUTION

BY WILL BASS

In the United States Constitution, Article 1 Section I gives Congress only those "legislative powers herein granted" and proceeds to list those permissible actions in Article I Section 8, while Section 9 lists actions that are prohibited for Congress. The vesting clause in Article II places no limits on the Executive branch, simply stating that, "The Executive Power shall be vested in a President of the United States of America."[6] The Supreme Court holds "The judicial Power" according to Article III, and it established the implication of Judicial review in Marbury vs Madison.[7] The federal government refers to the branches as "branches of government", while some systems use "government" to describe the executive. The Executive branch has attempted to claim power arguing for separation of powers to include being the Commander in Chief of a standing army since the Civil war, executive orders, emergency powers and security classifications since WWII, national security, signing statements, and the scope of the unitary executive.

Checks and Balances

To prevent one branch from becoming supreme, protect the "opulent minority" from the majority, and to induce the branches to cooperate, government systems that employ a separation of powers need a way to balance each of the branches. Typically this was accomplished through a system of "checks and balances", the origin of which, like separation of powers itself, is specifically credited to Montesquieu. Checks and balances allow for a system based regulation that allows one branch to limit another, such as the power of Congress to alter the composition and jurisdiction of the federal courts.

Legislative. (Congress)

Passes bills; has broad taxing and spending power; controls the federal budget; has power to borrow money on the credit of the United States. (may be vetoed by President, but vetoes may be overridden with a two-thirds vote of both houses)

Has sole power to declare war.

Oversees, investigates, and makes the rules for the government and its officers.

Defines by law the jurisdiction of the federal judiciary in cases not specified by the Constitution.

Ratification of treaties signed by the President and gives advice and consent to presidential appointments to the federal judiciary, federal executive departments, and other posts. (Senate only)

Has sole power of impeachment (House of Representative s) and trial of impeachments (Senate); can remove federal executive and judicial officers from office for high crimes and misdemeanors.

Executive. (President)

Is the commander-in-chief of the armed forces.

Executes the instructions of Congress.

May veto bills passed by Congress (but the veto may be overridden by a two-thirds majority of both houses)

Executes the spending authorized by Congress.

Declares states of emergency and publishes regulations and executive orders.

Makes executive agreements (does not require ratification) and signs treaties. (ratification requiring by two-thirds of the Senate)

Makes appointments to the federal judiciary, federal executive departments, and other posts with the advice and consent of the Senate. Has power to make temporary appointment during the recess of the Senate has the power

Continued on Page 45

A WORLD IN CHAOS

Randy English

"12 shot dead at 'Dark Knight Rises' screening in Aurora, Colorado."

"Rate of Killings Rises 38 Percent in Chicago in 2012"

"Mass Casualties After Shootings In Toronto And Tuscaloosa."

"4 Dead, 31 Wounded In Shootings This Weekend, Chicago."

"At least 9 wounded, 2 fatally, in shootings across city. Chicago."

These head lines, from a 30 day period in July of 2012 make us wonder what is happening to this world. What makes a person pick up a gun and kill innocent people? What is wrong in the United States, the land of the free, the land of plenty?

From an article in China-USA Trade Guide we see these statistics:

• The United States has the highest incarceration rate in the world and the largest total prison population on the entire globe.

• According to NationMaster.com, the United States has the highest percentage of obese people in the world.

• The United States has the highest divorce rate on the globe by a wide margin.

• The United States is tied with the UK for the most hours of television watched per person each week.

• The United States has the highest rate of illegal drug use on the entire planet.

• There are more car thefts in the United States each year than anywhere else in the world by far.

• There are more reported rapes in the United States each year than anywhere else in the world.

• There are more reported murders in the United States each year than anywhere else in the world.

• There are more total crimes in the United States each year than anywhere else in the world.

• The United States also has more police officers than anywhere else in the world.

What is wrong in the United States? Too many things to count. With the coming of the industrial age in the United States there was a pulling away from tradition. People left the farms to move to cities for better paying jobs. Once in the cities many isolated themselves for various reasons. Many stopped talking to their neighbors; some people today do not even know who their neighbors are. They replaced good manners with the "me first" attitude. They replaced religious values with "this is what I want."

Over time, this deliberate distancing, both physical and emotionally, has led to a numbing effect on people. If something does not affect them directly they tend to ignore it. We see this all the time when someone has a serious health problem and the neighbors walk past, noticing the pain the person is in, and then passing by without so much as a word of concern. It's no wonder that out of this indifference that some people carry the indifference to the extreme, to the point of killing other people. After all, they are not emotionally connected to them.

Then too there are the influences of TV, Music, Movies and Video games. Some people tend to play down these powerful stimulants. But they shouldn't. For example, think of a song that makes you happy, now one that makes you sad. If a song can change your mood simply by listening to it imagine playing a violent video game for hours, days, weeks or years. What influence could that have on a person who say has a mental instability, is reclusive, or has

anger issues?

Many of the killings this summer are black on black and gang related. Why do people form gangs? Why do they section off parts of cities and claim that territory and fight to the death for it. Why do the residents of those cities stand for it. Sure, now it's too late to stop it, but when it first started with just a few members, why didn't parents and other community members stop it?

Many reasons are given. Some say that it is lack of opportunity. But that is not the case. There have been too many who have made a good life for themselves without joining gangs and getting into drugs. Some say it is peer pressure. That one is certainly true. But the best antidote to peer pressure is good parenting. Schools are also to blame. Many of these gangs operate right inside of the public school systems. Schools should have a "zero-tolerance" for gangs. Schools, if need be, should have security to protect children.

Other reasons for killings are loss of jobs, depression, divorce, hate and so on. All of these reasons go back to one very basic problem. Selfishness. The person is so centered on their own situation that they stop caring about others. They think, "If I hurt, you're going to hurt too."

Then there are the few that want to make a name for themselves. Sure, they could do it the old fashioned way, by working hard, or helping others. But once again that self-centered thing comes in. They see killing as exciting and again, it's all about themselves. They don't care about the pain they inflict on others. After all, killing is glorified in movies, books, music and games.

So the next time you take your child to the store and they point at the latest video "murder" game, or the latest "murder" movie, or want that rap song that talks about "killing," do yourself and the rest of us a favor, tell them that killing is not fun and games! ∎

"Change does not roll in on the wheels of inevitability, but comes through continuous struggle.

Martin Luther King, Jr.

How Do you View Life?

If the question sounds strange to you then you're life is likely normal, or what people would call normal.

If you view life in a cynical light, you likely have been a victim of unfortunate circumstances.

If you view life as up-beat and positive, you are likely young.

If you view life as full of adventure you are free.

If you view life as hopeless, miserable, lacking meaning and purpose, you might be a Registered Sex Offender.

Where Has Our Personal Freedom Gone?

by Robert Wolfe

I think it is time to take a look at where our legislators are leading us. America has always been based on the concept that all men are free and there should be no barriers put up barring a person's freedom regardless of any defining characteristics that a person has. The most obvious examples are race, color, creed, or religion but there are others, also.

There are many historical examples of what has happened when caste systems are put into place. The most obvious is Nazi Germany, where millions of people were sorted out of the population and any group that was disliked had added restrictions and requirements placed on them. Eventually, this led to their murders. Not only the Jews but Romani (more commonly known in English by the exonym "Gypsies"), Sinti, Soviet prisoners of war, Polish and Soviet civilians, people with disabilities, Jehovah's Witnesses, and other political and religious opponents; which occurred regardless of whether they were of German or non-German ethnic origin. Using this definition, the total number of civilians murdered by the Nazis is between 10 million and 11 million (around 5.7 million Jews and a roughly equal number of non-Jews.

We all think about the pictures of people being loaded onto trains like cattle and taken to the concentration camps. But stop and think about what their lives must have been like before it got that far. Everyone had to carry papers with them continuously including children to show who they were and any official could stop them and ask for their papers. If they didn't have their papers or they were out of date they were imprisoned or worse.

Names were published in local papers if they were on the disfavored groups list. And if one member of a family was defined as a member of the disfavored group the entire family suffered from that stigma. They were denied jobs and places to live. They were forced to live in ghetto type surroundings. If they did own a business it was vandalized and eventually forced to shut down for lack of clients. If they worked for someone else and their employer found out that they were on the list they lost their jobs. People on the disfavored list could then be barred from certain types of employment. They were prohibited from using state hospitals. Public parks, libraries, and beaches were closed to them. There were communities that had signs outside their borders that literally said no Jews (or other disfavored groups) allowed. It took a World War to straighten out that mess, and millions of good people died because of what started out as registries based on bigotry and justified by saying it made society safer and protected the children.

People that believe in this type of law or even that this type of law is necessary would fit right in to the upper echelons of Nazi Germany. We have started to re-create the Nuremberg Laws from prewar Germany.

As Americans, we pride ourselves on the freedom that everyone in our country has. But today we too are creating caste's of people that we dislike; forcing them to register and constantly update their Information. Some communities have forced them out of their homes and made zones where they cannot live; they have forced them to put signs up in their yards or have license plates that shame them for something they have already paid for. Now our politicians are trying to force a more diverse group of people to be on those registries. If we saw this happening in another country, Americans would be outraged. We like to say that the least of our

people has the same freedoms as everyone else in this country. That is no longer true. We, as a country, have always had bigots and we have allowed ourselves to follow them; then later been ashamed of our actions. The most obvious examples are the way we treated Blacks, Hispanics and Asian. then what we did to the Japanese Americans during World War II, and of course what happened to people black listed during the McCarthy Era Right after World War II.

If, out of your hatred, self-righteousness, or bigotry, you believe that these types of laws are justifiable, then you do not understand what it is to be an American. You need to leave this country and go live somewhere else for a while. I would suggest North Korea, Pakistan, Iran, or any number of countries in Africa. Maybe then you would understand personal freedoms and how fragile and sacred they are. Any time you pass a law that takes away somebody else's personal freedoms you are shooting yourself in the foot and eventually you'll bleed to death

The Supreme Court began to overturn Jim Crow laws on constitutional grounds. It took nearly 50 years to overturn these bigoted laws that took away America's rights. The court held that a Kentucky law could not require residential segregation. The Supreme Court ruled segregation in interstate transportation to be unconstitutional, in an application of the commerce clause of the Constitution. The court held that separate facilities were inherently unequal in the area of public schools, outlawing Jim Crow in other areas of society as well, and slowly dismantled the state-sponsored segregation imposed by Jim Crow laws.

Along with Jim Crow laws, by which the state compelled segregation of the races, private parties such as businesses, political parties and unions created their own Jim Crow arrangements, barring disfavored citizens from buying homes in certain neighborhoods, from shopping or working in certain stores, from working at certain trades, etc. The Supreme Court outlawed some forms of private discrimination in which it held that restrictive covenants that barred sale of homes to blacks or Jews or Asians were unconstitutional, because they represented state-sponsored discrimination, in that they were only effective if the courts enforced them.

It took nearly 50 years to overturn these bigoted laws that took away America's rights.

It is difficult to estimate the number of victims of McCarthyism. The number imprisoned is in the hundreds, and some ten or twelve thousand lost their jobs. Many of those who were imprisoned, lost their jobs or were questioned by committees did in fact have a past or present connection of some kind with the Communist Party. But for the vast majority, both the potential for them to do harm to the nation and the nature of their communist affiliation were tenuous. Suspected homosexuality was also a common cause for being targeted by McCarthyism. The hunt for "sexual perverts"

(lesbians and gays), who were presumed to be subversive by nature, resulted in thousands being harassed and denied employment.

Since the time of McCarthy, the word McCarthyism has entered American speech as a general term for a variety of practices: aggressively questioning a person's patriotism or a person's character, making poorly supported accusations, or to discredit an opponent, subverting civil rights in the name of national security or group safety and the use of demagoguery* are all often referred to as McCarthyism. McCarthyism can also be synonymous with the term witch-hunt, both referring to mass hysteria and moral panic.

It seems in the light of history that only when they come for you will you realize that you should have stood up for the civil and equal rights of even those that you thought were the most despicable? By giving up their constitutional rights, you will lose your own and have nobody to blame but yourself.

Second-class citizen is an informal term used to describe a person who is systematically discriminated against within a state or other political jurisdiction, despite their nominal status as a citizen or legal resident there. While not necessarily slaves, second-class citizens have limited legal rights, civil rights, and economic opportunities, and are often subject to mistreatment or neglect at the hands of their putative superiors. Instead of being protected by the law, the law disregards a second-class citizen, or it may actually be used to harass them. Second-class citizenry is generally regarded as a violation of human rights. Typical impediments facing second-class

citizens include, but are not limited to, disenfranchisement, limitations on civil service, as well as restrictions on language, religion, education, freedom of movement and association, housing, and property ownership.

If you think you absolutely have to have registration and notification. Then it is the Legislator's duty to all the citizens of this country to set the laws down in such a way that only the less than 1% who have the probability of re-offending are placed on that list. Not a general catch-all for anybody who falls underneath the definition of a conviction for a crime. This is because we have to protect the Rights of the 99.9% of American citizens that will not re-offend. But recognize as the list gets smaller the damage to a person's life gets greater. If you put one person on that list who would have never re-offend then that person is murdered by some psychopath in the community because of his placement on the list or even worse if that person goes out and commits another crime, because he feels so hopeless and lost and so cut off from the community that he can only see himself as a terrible person with no other options. This will be a direct result of them being placed on the list. Then where is the blame to be placed for the loss of that person or their new victim? On the community, the legislators, and the persons designing the risk assessments, or possibly the therapists who helped in making the decisions? They must take part of the blame for the crimes. Before anyone is placed on a list the legislative body had best layout the rules very very carefully using

every tool at their disposal and find a very accurate way to determine if a person is absolutely going to re-offend because, as the Supreme Court has said time and time again, it is better to release a guilty person into the public than it is to convict an innocent one. The Supreme Court has even gone so far as to say it is better to release a mentally ill person into the community then to place a non-mentally ill person into a mental institution. That is what this country is all about—personal freedom that is not easily taken away or denied to all of its citizens.

we have to protect the Rights of the 99.9% of American citizens

American jurisprudence is consistent on the subject of punishing innocent people. The Supreme Court first commented on the issue in 1895, when the majority opinion in Coffin v. United States is cited. Virtually all of the Supreme Court-level guilty-men jurisprudence was created in the 1970s, starting with In re Winship (1970). The majority opinion in Winship stated, somewhat noncommittally, that "it is critical that the moral force of the criminal law not be diluted by a standard of proof that leaves people in doubt whether innocent men are being condemned." Justice Harlan's concurring opinion, through Athenian law, Trajan, Fortescue, Hale, and Blackstone all at once, to underscore the long history of the presumption of innocence, The Court revisited the issue in 1959 and established that "it is better, so the Fourth Amendment teaches, that the guilty sometimes go free than that citizens be subject to easy

arrest." was much stronger and has been more widely cited. "I view the requirement of proof beyond a reasonable doubt in a criminal case," Justice Harlan wrote, "as bottomed on a fundamental value determination of our society that it is far worse to convict an innocent man than to let a guilty man go free."

In 1829 a D.C. court cited Matthew Hale's 5 guilty men. The court also pointed out that if Hale's opinion had been required, "there can be no doubt that his patriotism would have prompted him to say, that it is better that ten guilty persons should escape punishment, than that any one of those rules of the common law which were adopted for the protection of the personal liberty and safety of the subject or citizen, should be abrogated."

Are such laws creating a caste systems really acceptable under our Constitution? U.S. v. Brown, 381 U.S. 437 (1965), U.S. v. Lovett 328 U.S. 303 (1946), and In re Yung Sing Hee (1888) establish bills of pains and penalties as punishment without trial, and included within the prohibitions of bills of attainder. The precedent that best reflects most of the original intention of the mandates is from Cummings v. Missouri, 71 U.S. 277 (1867). It states, "A bill of attainder, is a legislative act which inflicts punishment without judicial trial and includes any legislative act which takes away the life, liberty or property of a particular named or easily ascertainable person or group of persons because the legislature thinks them guilty of conduct which deserves punishment."

U.S. v. Lovett was a case historically relevant. It states:

"Legislative acts, no matter what their form, that apply either to named individuals or to easily ascertainable members of a group in such a way as to inflict punishment on them without a trial, are 'bills of attainder' prohibited under this clause. It would seem that from this, forcing people to register and have the community notified would fall into that category.

Further insight comes from examining several questions. Are bills of attainder and ex post facto laws disjunctive; is one a subset of the other, or do they overlap partially but not completely? Clearly, ex post facto laws are bills of attainder when they apply to the class of convicted persons and operate to increase the penalty, or likelihood of penalty, for them. Therefore, a class of persons convicted of something can be a suspect class for which, if a legislative act imposes a penalty on them, either after sentence is passed, or not as part of the sentence, that act is a bill of attainder.

Does it have to be a legislative act to be a bill of attainder or ex post facto law? No. Executive acts, purportedly under color of authority of a legislative act, such as regulations or administrative actions, can have the effect of a bill of attainder or ex post facto law, and therefore the act which authorizes the executive action, to the extent it authorizes that executive action, is a bill of attainder, and if the effect is retroactive, an ex post facto law.

The discussion during the Federal Convention limited bills of attainder and ex post facto laws to criminal disablements, but examined more carefully, they are actually just a complementary way to restate the requirement for due process in the Fifth Amendment, and include vested property as well as life and liberty. The Fifth Amendment says constitutional rights may only be deprived by judicial due process, and the prohibitions are against doing that by legislative process or executive process not based on a court order. Together, they emphasize that any disablement of a constitutional right must be by order of a court of competent jurisdiction upon petition and proof under due process protections of the rights of the defendant.

That they are insidiously taking away in very small bits and pieces everyone's rights...

Nearly 150 years ago in Cummings v. Missouri, 71 US 277 (1867), the Supreme Court struck a Missouri statute that required, among other persons, members of the clergy to swear a loyalty oath that they had not supported the government of the rebellion, lest they be forbidden from working. Because many citizens of Missouri were loyal to the Confederacy, they could not make such an attestation, lest they be subject to imprisonment for perjury. Though the language of the opinion does not help us clarify the question of "how to recognize a bill of attainder," the Court held that the Missouri law acted as an unconstitutional bill of attainder and wrote: "A bill of attainder, is a legislative act which inflicts punishment without judicial trial and includes any legislative act which takes away the life, liberty or property of a particular named or easily ascertainable person or group of persons because the legislature thinks them guilty of conduct which deserves punishment"

Violation of separation of powers: There is also a fundamental constitutional problem with officials of one sovereign imposing a penalty, either civil or criminal, based in whole or in part on the actions of officials of another sovereign. It is a violation of federalism and the separation of powers. Each branch and level of government is accountable solely to its own electors, and may not delegate authority to officials of another branch or level. In Lewis, what happens if the federal government convicts and sentences someone of the offense of carrying a firearm, on the basis of a conviction of a felony in a state court, and then the state offense is pardoned or overturned on appeal? It simply does not work, constitutionally, for the decisions of a state court to determine whether an act is a federal crime. That applies not only to state criminal proceedings, but to things like protective orders, competency hearings and commitment orders, indictments, arrests, issuance of licenses or permits, or any other official action

There are ways to fight and stop these registration laws. Americans must come to realize how onerous these laws are. That they are insidiously taking away in very small bits and pieces everyone's rights guaranteed under the Constitution. Rights people have fought, bled, and died for. If you believe in this country and what it stands for, the time is now to stop this madness and bring back all Americans rights before this country turns into another Nazi Germany.

*Demagogy or demagoguery is a

strategy for gaining political power by appealing to the prejudices, emotions, fears, vanities and expectations of the public—typically via impassioned rhetoric and propaganda, and often using nationalist, populist or religious themes. Though this definition emphasizes the use of lying and falsehoods, skilled demagogues often need to use only special emphasis by which an uncritical listener will be led to draw the desired conclusion themselves. ∎

Former Sex Offenders and Employment

by Randy English

In many places unemployment among Registered Sex Offenders is very high. Often the problem can be residency or proximity restrictions. Other times it is that employers do not want their address listed on the public registry for fear of vigilante actions, or losing customers. For whatever the reasons, unemployment of former offenders is costing taxpayers lots of money.

When a person is unemployed they have no alternative but to turn to government funded programs for financial aid. From food stamps to disability programs, former offenders are lining up to cash in because they have been virtually kicked out of the work force.

But some who deal with registered former offenders have a different outlook. Sgt. Brad Brown of the Carroll County, Maryland, Sheriff's Office said, "It is a bit of a hurdle for some employers to get over that conviction of hiring a sex offender. However, the thing is, if they can do the job and are not a danger to anyone at the business and the public in general, then why not?"

This statement comes from someone who deals with former offenders daily. If these registrants were the danger that the public perceives would this officer be recommending hiring them? No, he would not. He goes on to say, "I find the majority of people on the registry don't want to violate any of the registry requirements, and don't want to violate the law period," Brown said. "Most of them are compliant just like in society. Most people in society obey most laws."

So the next time you have the opportunity to hire someone who is qualified for the job, has a good track record for employment and is a registered former offender, please hire that person. You may well find that they will be the best employee you ever had. ∎

100,000 UNREGISTERED SEX OFFENDERS!

by Randy English

You will hear this statistic quoted many times when new legislation is promoted against former sex offenders. This huge number forms the basis for more stringent laws based on fear not on fact.

So let's look at this number for a moment. Where did it come from? No one seems to be able to quote any accurate source. The truth is the number was just pulled out of thin air. So what are the facts and how can we find the actual number?

Using the sweeps conducted by local law enforcement in cooperation with Federal Marshals, we can glimpse the number more accurately. Many factors come into play. Areas with the most stringent residency restriction have the highest number of absconders. After all, no one wants to live under a bridge. Many areas have 0% absconders. These are usually rural areas and states where there are less registration requirements. If we look at the numbers, we will find that in areas that have residency restrictions to the extent that there are virtually no places for former offenders to live inside a home, the absconder percentages in those areas vary from 10% to roughly 14%. The numbers are not the norm, they are the extreme. In most areas the percentages seem to be around 6%. But given that the Marshals only target areas will large populations of registrants, the exact numbers are virtually unknown.

But let's take an average of 5% which is inordinately high for a national average. 5% of 750,000 equals 37,500 absconders. As I said, this number is much higher than current statistics bear out.

At any rate the misleading 100,000 unregistered sex offenders is misleading, or is it? Please notice that the quote does not say, 100,000 absconders. It says "100,000 unregistered sex offenders." Is that true? No, the number of unregistered sex offenders is far higher than that. But these are not people that the Marshals service can track down and arrest because they are not hiding. These are people who served their time long ago and do not have a duty of registering. These people are protected by the Constitution. They did their time and are now free to live their lives. But organizations like The National Center for Missing & Exploited Children and many legislators are pushing for the removal of constitutional protections for former sex offenders. These are the people who are putting forth the false statement "100,000 unregistered sex offenders."

Removal of Constitutional Protections and its Effect on the Public

If successful, legislators will bend, tear or destroy the constitution so that all former sex offenders will be forced to register. Some people feel this would be a good thing. But will it.? No. It will be the beginning of ultimate tyranny. Once a law like that is passed and if it is approved by the courts, it forms what is called case law. What this means is that the public in general will have to live with the same loss of constitutional rights of whom that law was targeting. If the public protests stating that the law was not meant to remove the rights of anyone except former offenders, the government will trot out the case law and the courts will back the removal of those rights for all American citizens.

So the next time you hear the quote "100,000 unregistered sex offenders," remember, someone is trying to frighten you into giving up "your" Constitutional rights. ∎

Food for Thought

by Penn Greene

Tell Congress that the Adam Walsh Act (AWA) and the Sex Offender Registration Act (SORNA) is illegal and unconstitutional.

Tell Congress that these laws are misrepresented as civil law with vindictive, retaliatory and punitive action that clearly offends our Constitutional rights as citizens of the United States of America, and is a disturbing, offensive affront to the supreme law of the land "Our Constitution of the United States"!

It is my contention that the Adam Walsh Act (AWA) and the Sex Offender Registration Act (SORNA) are, in fact, a life sentence of imprisonment, in addition to lifelong humiliation, degradation and subjugation (a form of slavery) outside of prison (The Constitution of the United States, Article I, Section 9, paragraph 3 provides that: "No Bill of Attainder or ex post facto Ex-post Facto Law will be passed.") long after a court sentence was completed and satisfied as ordered punishment..

"The Bill of Attainder Clause was intended not as a narrow, technical (and therefore soon to be outmoded) prohibition, but rather as an implementation of the separation of powers, a general safeguard against legislative exercise of the judicial function or more simply - trial by legislature." U.S. v. Brown, 381 U.S. 437, 440 (1965).

Ex post facto is an adjective affecting a previous act, after, after the act is committed, after the fact, afterward, at a later period, at a later time, at a subsequent period, at a succeeding time, directly after, following in time, later, later in time, retroactive, thereafter

Additionally, it should go without saying that our United States Constitutional 8th Amendment expresses protection from cruel and unusual punishment as:

Such punishment as would amount to torture or barbarity, any cruel and degrading punishment not known to the common law or any fine, penalty, confinement, or treatment that is so disproportionate to the offense as to shock the moral sense of the community.

Last but not least, our Fourteenth Amendment of our United States Constitution is supposed to prevent states from denying its citizens certain fundamental rights that are deemed essential to the concepts of equality or liberty, including the right to autonomy, dignity and self determination.

So you see! There are 3 distinct Constitutional laws trampled on by our Federal and State Governments. This behavior by our governing bodies will eventually extend directly into your freedoms if you do not take a stand and stop this illegal behavior from our legislators who act with total abandonment to our legal and civil rights. ■

> "Never be afraid to raise your voice for honesty and truth and compassion against injustice and lying and greed. If people all over the world...would do this, it would change the earth."
>
> William Faulkner

Would YOU Participate in a March on Washington, D.C.?

Many of us feel it may be the only way to get our message heard.
We realize it will take money, planning and courage but many of us are talking about a march. If you would be seriously interested in marching with us in Washington, D.C. Please contact any on the reform groups including; RSO Advocacy, SOSEN WAR, RSOL or Texas Voices.

WE NEED YOU!

Keeps up with

RSO Advocacy Magazine

visit

www.rso-advocacy.org

Open Letter To SCOTUS

Another year has gone by and, as predicted, those citizens who are publicly shamed and marked, much like those similar citizens of 75 years ago in Germany, have lost more of their Constitutionally Protected Rights in the esoteric name of "Public safety", again, very much like the reasoning used 75 years ago in Nazi Germany's Courts.

The continual flood of new restrictions and sanctions that come almost daily since this Court ruled in Doe-v-Smith, 01-729, in 2003 continue to erode the very Constitution Rights this Court is purportedly tasked with protecting. The Supreme Court granted certiorari and then reversed the Ninth Circuit's decision finding that the Registry DID NOT impose any "punitive restraints" in violation of the Ex Post Facto Clause of the Constitution nor was it restrictive or supervisory in intent, but that is was purely a Public Safety Regulatory scheme.

Is it a Regulatory Scheme with criminal penalties and consequences, some many times more severe than the original charges carried? It was deemed not to be an Ex Post Facto Law or punishment but a Public Safety Regulatory Scheme for several very basic key reasons in that opinion;

1 - Registrants' convictions were already a matter of Public Record. (*) Yes, and if they only posted the public information from our arrest and conviction, that would be fine. But our current photos, home addresses and employment information, TODAY, IS NOT PART OF THAT PUBLIC RECORD. Nor is our phone number, email addresses, and hundreds of other bits of personal information we are now being force to divulge for public dissemination.

2 - Registrants have an extremely high rate of recidivism. (*) NOT TRUE AND A BLANTANT DISREGARD FOR THE FACTS, IF NOT A LIE TOLD TO SIMPLY INFLAME THIS COURTS MORAL COMPASS! This Court was "lead" to believe this myth via misquoted and outdated information that, today, has been refuted and disproved time and time again. One in fact by the Dept. of Justice itself puts that figure at less than 4%, second lowest rate of any offender, and finding Sex Offenders are the least likely to re-offend sexually.

3 - From Doe-v-Smith - "The record in this case contains no evidence that the Act has led to substantial occupational or housing disadvantages for former sex offenders..." (*) this misperception by the court needs little explanation, if any, to disprove these myths. Simply searching for news articles from Florida and California, just to mention two locations, and one will see Registered Offenders now being forced to live under bridges and being forced into jobless and homeless nomadic lives because of the Registry. Please, not that many of these registrants have places to live and careers. However due to the registry they are barred, by law, from living in their own homes or working at jobs that they are specifically trained for.

On 6-28-2010 Rep. Jim McDermott (WA-7) introduced HR 5618 "Restoration of Emergency Unemployment Compensation Act of 2010" with an amendment to that Act to ensure that benefits under this Act are NOT provided to any individual convicted of a sex offense against a minor (as such terms are defined in section 111 of the Sex Offender Registration and Notification Act (42 U.S.C. 16911).

On 5-13-2010 Rep. Barney Frank (MA-4) introduced HR 5297 "Small Business Jobs and Credit Act of 2010" with an amendment denying loans to the principals of such businesses that have been convicted of a sex offense against a minor (as such terms are defined in section 111 of the Sex Offender Registration and Notification Act (42 U.S.C. 16911).

Then there is "The FHA Reform Act of 2010" (HR 5072) where Rep. Edwards of Texas proposed Amendment 12. In essence it required that "individuals to certify that they have not been convicted of a sex offense against a minor in order to get an FHA mortgage."

These three bills, and many others like them, are clearly discriminately punitive in intent solely to punish and deny Former Offenders any legitimate opportunity to rejoin society. One will notice that

none of the Amendments to these Bills include Drunk Drivers who kill more children each year than any single group of offenders, much less Former Sex Offenders. Even someone who is convicted of murdering a child would be eligible for extended unemployment benefits, an FHA Mortgage and/or a Small Business Loan while an public Registrant would be denied any chance to live the American Dream much less a second chance at life which this country has long stood for both here and around the world.

As for "Occupational" restrictions, we have seen numerous laws passed to restrict where Former Offenders can now work. Many proposed laws are in the works right now, which if passed will deny Former Offenders any opportunities of working in any fields that "might" put them even in the vicinity of a child. In many States Former Offenders can't even hold Professional Positions like Real-Estate Sales, Taxi Driver, etc.. And let's not forget, "No Extended Unemployment Benefits" when we do lose any job we might have found by the Grace of God.

4 - From Doe-v-Smith - "...the record contains no indication that an in-person appearance requirement has been imposed on any sex offender subject to the Act." (*) Not only do we have to make in-person appearances, we are required to report to Local Law Enforcement regularly and subject to supervisory interviews and questioning as to our private lives and actions. Failure to comply carries severe Criminal Penalties and consequences, and again, some of them many times more severe than the original offensecarried that lead to one being on the Registry. Some are under virtual "House Arrest" every 90 days while we await verification. We can't leave town or go on vacations at those times, no exceptions. And if we do leave at other times, we are now required to notify the State that we are leaving, where we are going and staying, and when we will be back. Connecticut is even considering a law that "Mandates" that Former Offenders must submit an application to the State at least 48 hours BEFORE they enter the State with a complete criteria of their visit even if they are just driving threw to another State. Nevada and several other States now mandate Registration if a Former Offender even crosses the State Line when traveling, even if the Registrant is not stopping in that State.

5 - From Doe-v-Smith - "...offenders subject to the Alaska statute are free to move where they wish and to live and work as other citizens, with no supervision." (*) They are NOT free to move, travel, live and work as other citizens any longer. The Registry of today is all about Supervision and control. The Government tells former offenders where they can live and work, where they can move and travel to, and all of this requires the Registrant to report to the State and seek approval, and some must seek State approval BEFORE they take any action. It is now necessary for a registrant to get permission to leave the country. No other class of people in the United States has to ask permission to leave.

Restrictions placed on many offenders today are more severe and restrictive than those they had to comply with while on Supervised Parole or Probation many years ago before Doe-v-Smith. Note bullet point #3 for more similar points.

We wonder if the Honored members of this court, would still hold Doe-v-Smith as a Constitutional Regulatory Scheme with severe Criminal Penalties today considering the plethora of Politically motivated draconian and oppressive "Criminal" laws being passed to pacify the fear and hysterical cries of the nation's lynch mobs for revenge against Former Offenders?

Doe-v-Smith is the flag of authority waved as Constitutional validation of every draconian law passed even though many of these laws far exceed the limits this Court set in Doe-v-Smith.

Almost daily, a new law is passed that uses the Registry scheme and the fear and hysteria it has incited, to curtail the rights and freedoms of Former Offenders. Many are being sent to prison to serve severe criminal penalties for a Civil Violation of this Regulatory Scheme for nothing more than a technical violation due to an oversight or just plainly unaware of one of the thousands of limitations and restrictions waiting out there to ensnare an unformed Offender who had no real intent to commit any crime, excuse me, "Regulatory Violation". Some even for life for a violation of this "Regulatory" scheme. They are being forced to move from family homes and property without due process to sleep in cars and under bridges. Those

that had employment are being terminated with little to no hope of finding another job as vigilantes use the Registry information to harass employers and businesses who hire former offenders trying to give them a chance to rejoin society as a productive taxpaying citizen.

Fear, Myth and Hysteria concerning Former Offenders are the fodder of Politicians seeking the media spot-light and votes. The Sex Offender Issue is the trough for the media headlines to obtain ratings. I won't go on as I am confident you are very aware of the climate this decision, Doe-v-Smith, has created and the Political crutch it has become for every Politian seeking office on the "Former Sex Offender's Back".

It is a climate of death and destruction as well. Records clearly show a steep increase in Registered Former Sex Offender (RFSO) murders related to the Registry that directly correlates with the 2003 Doe-v-Smith ruling. Over 200 RFSOs have been murdered in the last seven years. How long before RFSOs become the "Strange Fruit" that Billie Holiday sang about during another time when society deemed another class of citizens less deserving of their Civil Rights much like today with Former Sex Offenders?

How many innocent people have been killed such as the wife of a Registered Former Offender who died when vigilantes set his house on fire using address information from the Registry Website? The registrant escaped, but his wife did not. Then there is the 12 year old boy killed in Florida when Vigilantes fired shots at his father inside his home, missing the registrant and hitting the boy in the head. Or those mistaken or accused of being a Sex Offender and killed by vigilantes. There may be more that we are unaware of as Law Enforcement has been downplaying Sex Offender murders since the incident in Washington State when an individual, using the Registry Website, obtained information and addresses of registrants, and then posed as an FBI agent and killed two Offenders and was looking for a third when he was caught. Quoted from the news interviews with Washington authorities... "We don't want to bring too much attention to these murders for fear of a sympathetic backlash that might endanger the Registry."

How many Registered Former Offenders

have to be "Lynched" before it stops? Probably the saddest part of all this is a statement we read in one of the local newspapers in Maine when a Legislator commented on the Maine State Supreme Court ruling in 2007 concerning the Registry being punitive and similar to pillory of old. He stated that "the Court had no business telling the Legislature its business."

The Williams case in the Ohio Supreme Court bears out the fact that the registry in now punitive. The court states in part; Some factors pertaining to the statutory scheme governing sex offenders, however, suggested that the statutory scheme was punitive. First, the procedures for registration and classification of sex offenders were placed within Ohio's criminal code, R.C. Title 29. Second, failure to comply with certain registration requirements subjected a sex offender to criminal prosecution. R.C. 2950.99.

When we were in school they taught us that there were three (3) branches of our constitutionally formed Government, the Executive, the Legislative, and the Judiciary. All designed by our founding fathers in order to assure the proper checks and balances of power, and to protect the rights of the people. Even the Rights of scoundrels.

We will leave you again with this wisdom below considering the tough job ahead of you on this topic. Perhaps these words of wisdom will help; "Judges ... rule on the basis of law, not public opinion, and they should be totally indifferent to pressures of the times." Justice Warren E. Burger Chief Justice, U. S. Supreme Court "He that would make his own liberty secure, must guard even his enemy from oppression; for if he violates this duty, he establishes a precedent which will reach to himself." - Thomas Paine (1737-1809), Dissertation on First Principles of Government, 1795.

"The trouble with fighting for human freedom is that one spends most of one's time defending scoundrels. For it is against scoundrels that oppressive laws are first aimed, and oppression must be stopped at the beginning if it is to be stopped at all." - H. L. Mencken

Respectfully and Sincerely,
A Registered Former Sex Offender

IF IT JUST SAVES ONE CHILD

by H. Niemand

> The most hypocritical of those that use this line are politicians.

"If it just saves one child" is the catch phrase used by those who would make anyone with any type of sex offense on their record, social and economic pariahs.

It's a good thing though that the word "If" starts the phrase. This is because there is no proof that the Sex Offender Registry or any other sex offender law has ever saved one child or adult.

The Sex Offender Registration and Notification Act (SORNA), which contains the Adam Walsh Act (AWA), are costing the Federal Government millions to maintain and enforce. In addition, each state that adopts it will spend millions to maintain and enforce it. This will result in a cost of many billions of tax dollars in this ongoing process.

The most hypocritical of those that use this line are politicians. They talk about saving children by spending tax dollars for laws, while cutting funding to programs that actually do help and maybe save children from all types of abuse. They vote for prisons and vote against programs that just might keep a child from despair.

Many of the after school programs that kept children off the streets and give latch key kids a place to go other than an empty house, have been de-funded because there is no money.

Pre-school programs that gave children a head-start in school and working parents a safe place for their children when they go to work, have been de-funded because there is no money.

School lunch programs that gave many children their one-good-meal a day have been de-funded because there is no money.

Schools themselves are under-funded so that education of our youth is at risk. Liberal Arts such as civics, social studies, art and music are no longer taught in many schools because there is no money.

Cash strapped states are unable to gain federal matching funds for their SCHIP (State Children's Health Insurance Program) programs because there is no money. Also, SCHIP is a block grant with a fixed annual funding level. Consequently, the federal SCHIP funding that states receive has not been keeping pace with the rising cost of health care or population growth.

Services for children are being cut drastically in every state, county, city and town across the nation because there is no money.

Departments of Children and Families are having staff cut to the bone drastically reducing home visits for at risk children protect everyone are being laid off because there is no money.

Police Officers who protect everyone are being laid off because there is no money.

Fire Fighters protect everyone are being laid off because there is no money.

But yet, every state finds millions of dollars to implement and enforce more and more ineffective registry laws using the refrain, "If it just saves one child" while they let millions suffer because there is no money! ∎

The Gary Blanton Story
Loving Husband and Father

As told by his wife, Leslie Blanton

The emotion, anguish and anger which were caused by the death of Gary Blanton can only be understood through the words and tears of his wife, Leslie.

This is the story of true love, which was needlessly destroyed by the heinous acts of a cunning murderer and a callous legal system that is aiding vigilantes to target registrants as their victims. It is also the story of a judgmental society that assigns a label to a person, never allowing them to grow beyond that label.

Leslie explains "In 2004, I met Gary at the home of a mutual friend." She recalls that Gary kept looking at her and then boldly walked up and asked, "Are you dating anyone?" When she responded that she was not, he asked, "Would you date me?" Leslie voice lifted for a moment as she recalled what she said in response. "What? Are you 12 years old?" He laughed and said, "No, I'm nineteen." She responded, "Well, I'm 20 then."

Leslie was actually 27 years old when she met the man she lovingly called, 'Daddy Detroit.' It was one of those love-at-first-sight moments, at least for Gary; for very soon after that he told Leslie, that he would one day marry her. He also told her about the crime that landed him on the Sex Offender Registry.

You see, Gary was what some people call, "one of those people." When he was 17 years old he had sexual contact with another teen. Some would call this dating in our modern times; others call it hooking-up. The law calls it a sex offense and places the person (usually the male) on the Sex Offender Registry for this common transgression.

Kate Logan and Randy English of RSO Advocacy Magazine, sat down with Leslie to talk to her about the tragic event that took her husband, the love of her life, away from her. It was difficult for us to listen to this story and

"He was a great father. He loved his boys so much. They were his world."

we can only express, that words alone can never fully communicate the devastating loss that she and her children have had to endure. Listening to Leslie talk brings the hearer into a story of true love and honest friendship. The story of a caring and loving father and a system that is greatly responsible for his death. We invite you to listen to Leslie's expressions in the following interview.

Leslie, when did you and Gary marry? "We were married in 2008."

What was Gary like? "Gary was amazing and giving! He would give you the shirt off his back if he thought that you needed it. He was just that way. He helped so many people. He was always thinking of others before himself.

"And he was a great father. He loved his boys so much. They were his world.

"He was also kind of a hillbilly at times. He liked video games and he was stubborn now and then. But he was a loving man, kind and generous, that's the Gary I want people to remember"

Were you worried about marrying a registered sex offender? "No, I knew Gary, I wasn't worried about him. But I didn't know that his being on the Sex Offender Registry was going to be so difficult for us. I mean…he couldn't get a job and then there were places he couldn't go, live. He couldn't even go to church

Interview conducted by Kate Logan
Article written by Randy English

with me and our children. This affected me also. I have been treated badly by people because of 'our' being on the registry.

"When our children were born, one of the children was born with Down's Syndrome. Gary was so worried about him; he stayed with the baby all the time. Then the hospital found out that Gary was on the registry. A security guard came, told Gary he had to leave the hospital." Leslie began to cry for the memory was so painful. "He was not even allowed to see his OWN child. Gary had to go home and leave me there with the baby. He was so hurt. We went to that hospital for help and then the hospital was horrible to us. Gary was not a danger to anyone and no one would listen. They see the label and that's all they see. I hate that label, no one should have that label!"

Leslie, when was Gary put on the registry? "2002, he was 17. He told me about it and then he started to look worried, waiting to see my response. But it wasn't as big a deal as people make it out to be. Kids do that all the time. I told him, "I still love you.""

How did Gary's family react to his being on the registry? "Some in his family wouldn't talk about it, but it was always there, 'like an elephant in the middle of the room.' His sister found out about it last year and called him. He felt bad that she called to ask about it.

After that she didn't call him again."

How did your family treat Gary? "My dad's a pastor. He said, 'Everyone has a right to be treated like a human. As long as Gary treats you good, that's all that matters to me. Does he treat you good?' I answered, 'Yes, he treats me very good.' Dad said, 'That's good enough for me.'"

Did Gary have friends that turned on him because of being on the registry? "Yes, and it hurt him..; but that's when you find out who your real friends are. They just sort of stopped including him in things."

Did he have friends that stood by him? "Oh, yes! One of his best friends has stood by him through everything. He said that some people would say, 'he's a sex offender.' His reply was, 'I don't care, I love Gary like a brother.'"

Leslie now talked about Gary, some things she wanted us to tell people about him. She told us about how even before their children were born, even before they started to develop in her womb, "Gary would read to them, 'so they will learn my voice.'" Through this interview we came to understand that to Gary, Leslie and his children were his world; which is why the next part of this story is so reprehensible.

Last year, after coming home to find their baby sitter eager to leave as soon as she could, Gary realized that something was wrong. The child was crying uncontrollably and in obvious pain. Gary and Leslie rushed the child to the hospital. It was determined that the child had suffered a broken arm. Gary's parole officer was summoned and soon Gary was being arrested and charged for breaking the arm. No investigation was needed to bring these charges, after all he was a sex offender, he had to have done it.

After that an investigation was started and Gary was ordered to leave the home; this put a great hardship on the family. They were already in a bad situation what with all the restrictions from the registry, now Gary had to find a place to live that didn't cost too much.

Enter longtime friend Patrick Drum. Drum offered Gary a place to live that was almost too good to be true. The price was more than right and Gary moved in.

This is the string of events that led to the murder of loving husband and caring father, Gary Blanton. A rushed judgment from a "system" that looks at ones past and ignores the facts, led to this murder. How can we say that? Because after his death, Gary was cleared of all wrongdoing in the case involving the child's broken arm. Gary was innocent. He should have been home with his family, not in the home of a murderer. But in the eyes of those who accused, arrested and charged Gary, he had to be guilty because he was a SEX OFFENDER! They were wrong and we feel strongly that they bear a great part of the responsibility for his death.

We are unable to talk about the actual murder in this article for legal reasons, all we can say is that it was obviously planned and carried out by a conniving psychopath.

Drum has spoke in court and has been quoted stating that he, "Hates sex offenders." That he wanted to kill more sex offenders. Yet still he asked, lured, Gary Blanton to his home and offered to rent it at a cost that was far below normal. We will let the reader draw their own conclusions regarding this.

We asked Leslie how the public had treated her before the murders. "When people first met us everything was fine, normal. But when they found out that Gary was on the registry they would exclude us from most everything. Some people called him a 'pedo'. That's not true; Gary was never charged with or even accused of a crime that would include a prepubescent child."

Then we wanted to know how the public has reacted after the murder, after all, the public rallies around wives and children whose husbands have been murdered, right? "I have been harassed, people hiding in the bushes across the street, taking pictures of my home.

"When I went to the court house, with my two boys, a man called out to me, 'Hey, you're the wife of the pedo. He's dead right? He is dead.' One of my boy's, little Gary Jr. started crying and said, 'Daddy dead? Daddy dead.' We left the building. People are so cruel. Sure my children are little but they understand more than people think. The things people say in front of my kids is just not right." We agree and they should not say it to you either. Society has become cruel. They point at sex offenders as the bad guys, but their own conduct is reprehensible.

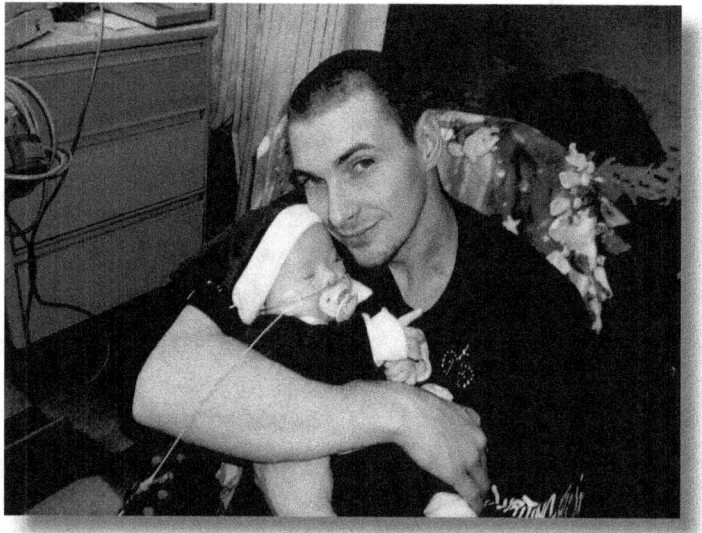

Leslie, have there been other incidences? "Yes, many. I have been harassed on Facebook. This is a difficult time for me and to have to read comments like, 'he deserved to die, and calling Drum 'a hero,' and saying they need to 'kill all of them.' And the government allows this kind of hate, encourages it by the use of a public 'hit list!' People are sick. I also had to change my phone number because sick people called me all hours of the night. I called the police about some

of this and they said I shouldn't worry about it. I told them that ,'I think I do have reason to worry, my husband was just murdered by a psychopath, a person with that same attitude as those who are now stalking me have, there are more of them out there, this is going to happen again!'"

RSO Advocacy Magazine agrees with Leslie, after all, some websites are still listing Gary's name and address as a sex offender.

www.offendex.com is a for-profit website and not for public safety, and right now this website is putting Leslie's family in danger. We hope that an attorney will come forward and offer to sue this website and any others that are still listing Gary's name.

Leslie, do you think there should be a sex offender registry? "No, well for law enforcement, sure they may need it, but they already have it. They have the records for everyone convicted of any crime. But for the public, no, there should be no public registry. It's just a 'hit list.'"

RSO Advocacy Magazine agrees with Leslie, the public registry has proved to be ineffective for stopping repeat offenses. After all, registered sex offenders have a very low re-offense rate. The real danger for children is not lurking on the "hit list," it's from people already known to the child.

The public registry has proved to be most effective as a tool for vigilantes. They use it to harass, to threaten, vandalize, beat and even murder those publicly listed on the "hit list" known as the Sex Offender Registry. All too often the family and friends of those on the "hit list" also become targets of vigilante ignorance. Leslie has seen all of this first hand. She has been left without her best friend, the love of her life. These innocent children have been robbed of their father. They will never know him. Leslie said, "We were supposed to grow old together, we were supposed to see our children grow and sit on the front porch together watching our grand children. Now that won't happen. Gary won't see his children grow and he won't know his grandchildren and the public registry is to blame. Gary paid for the 'crime' he did the time, the punishment, which should have been the end of it. I'm in this fight to end the registry for everyone who is listed on the public 'hit list.'" ∎

"When I was a boy of fourteen, my father was so ignorant I could hardly stand to have the old man around. But when I got to be twenty-one, I was astonished at how much he had learned in seven years."

Mark Twain

Separation - Continued

to grant "reprieves and pardons for offenses against the United States, except in cases of impeachment."

Judicial. (Supreme Court)

Determines which laws Congress intended to apply to any given case.

Exercises judicial review, reviewing the constitutionality of laws.

Determines how Congress meant the law to apply to disputes.

Determines how a law acts to determine the disposition of prisoners.

Determines how a law acts to compel testimony and the production of evidence.

Determines how laws should be interpreted to assure uniform policies in a top-down fashion via the appeals process, but gives discretion in individual cases to low-level judges. The amount of discretion depends upon the standard of review, determined by the type of case in question. ∎

Federal judges serve for life. ∎

Hacker to hacker. Unseen consequences.

A white hat's perspective in the dark world of the black hats known as Anonymous.

by Nicholas Maietta (nick@computer-hacker.net)

You'd have to live under a big rock, or at least somehow magically avoid all the news websites over the last couple of years especially, to not learn about the huge corporations and governmental agencies whose websites were defaced, taken offline or data extracted from the databases behind them. The biggest names most of us use everyday, such as Google, Facebook and Twitter have all fell victim at one time or another to the digital instructions and tasks perpetuated by these faceless hackers, crackers and script kiddies. There is one group of such hackers, crackers and script kiddies that have caught my attention, and the attention of people from all over our planet. This group is called Anonymous.

Anonymous is known for doing dirty deeds. They take down websites, they deface many and in many cases they managed to reach into databases and extract data and dump it publicly. This is their nature. They say they are leaderless, but they have only a handful of organizers and to me, that make thems leaders. They work together mostly, but sometimes alone. They share knowledge about their efforts, and they are highly politically motivated. They had a huge problem and they found a guaranteed way to mitigate that problem.

You see, most people don't like hackers in general. In the public's eye, hackers are generally bad for computers and networks. Those who understand the difference between white and black hackers know that this group in question are the bad, and not all hackers are the same. But Anonymous has decided to use the tried and true method of winning the support of those who previously thought of them as bad. It comes in the same style that many politicians are known for in most states. Target the "child molesters".

Operation Pedo Chat #OpPedoChat commenced on July 8th of this year. They promised to take down websites that they deemed to be worthy of taking down. In reviewing the first list they published, I was pretty glad to see they were targeting some pretty tough to kill websites. Most of the websites listed appear to be hosted in countries outside the jurisdiction of the United States. Our government cannot legally, or technically take down or remove access to some of the websites on the list. Some were definitely hosted within the United States and steps could have been taken legally to take those websites down.

All Bullies and Vigilanties will at some point have unintended consequences, here are some in which innocent suffer as a result. First, they forgot that most websites shared the physical hardware and software resources of other websites and services, belonging to people and businesses that have no connection to the website on the target list. These people become victims when they lose a client because they couldn't effectively communicate via email, or when the website they own can no longer process transactions that keep that business alive. When Anonymous takes down a website, they take the server with it and everything it has on it. It's a bucket of white out on a misspelled word when all that was needed was a dab. Furthermore, by rallying the support and participation of the general public, they put some Web Owners lives in danger of complete ruin.

Additionally, by breaking into databases and then dumping and deleting records, they destroy the very evidence needed to prosecute the website's operators if it ever did get turned over to law enforcement.

Most members, like that of Anonymous, are not good at covering their tracks online when participating in these distributed denial of service

style attacks will and regularly do, find themselves in federal prison. The kingpins of the operation continue to operate on Twitter and post their messages on Pastebin. Why has Twitter refused to take down their account?

Well, the way I see it, Anonymous, collectively has taken Twitter offline in the past and could threaten or bully them again if Anonymous doesn't get what they want.

The worst part of all this is the media's inability or unwillingness to fully check out the websites in the "target list". One website I am hosting was targeted, because of someone in Anonymous making a false accusation about the motive of the websites. It was finally taken off the target list after being attacked and only after the website's operator agreed to put up a strong message saying they support the group Anonymous.

"...
Greetings Anon and Thank you for all the Wonderful work you are doing to take down the Pedo's and anyone that will condone Child Sexual Abuse.
Please take into consideration that our website is not a Legitimate Target, we are an Activists Organization fighting unfair laws and oppression.
We are actually on your side standing against Child Sexual Abuse.
Thank you and please keep up the good work.
** bows to the master **
.."

I don't know about you, but I really hate bullies. I know I worked for free over the last few days defending my digital assets and the assets of my clients over a false assumption that we were hosting a website belonging to a pro-pedophila website when that was not the case at all. I still can't seem to get over the hypocrisy of them accessing the child pornography themselves. I am also willing to bet that if some of these people are caught, huge stashes of the child porn will be found on some hard drives, all in the name of protecting children when in fact, it was to take the heat off them so they can continue to hack away.

Could it be that this stunt was intended to rally the publics favor? If this is true, then they were using the same tactic politicians use to gain popularity. Their success bares witness to several online comments urging them on and praising them for their efforts. Time will only tell if they become the accepted online Vigilante. ∎

"If aliens are watching us through telescopes, they're going to think the dogs are the leaders of the planet.

If you see two life forms, one of them's making a poop, the other one's carrying it for him, who would you assume is in charge?"

Jerry Seinfeld

"A citizen of America will cross the ocean to fight for democracy, but won't cross the street to vote in a national election."

Bill Vaughan

The Supreme Court Received False or Inaccurate Information

by Will Bass and Al Lynne

Here is a Beautiful piece of information regarding how the Supreme Court was influenced with manipulated information. This is worth the time and consideration because most of us who are in the Reform Movement are well aware of the statistical and scientific information proving that Sex Offenders have a low re-offense rate.

Now if this information was avalible during the 2003 Smith vs. Doe supreme Court hearing, and there were false or misleading statements, or even information withheld upon reason for the need for a registry, it would have been a much different outcome.

U.S. official cites misconduct in Japanese American internment cases acting Solicitor Gen. Neal Katyal says one of his predecessors, Charles Fahy, deliberately hid from the Supreme Court a military report that Japanese Americans were not a threat in World War II.

May 24, 2011|By David G. Savage, Washington Bureau.

Reporting from Washington — Acting Solicitor Gen. Neal Katyal, in an extraordinary admission of misconduct, took to task one of his predecessors for hiding evidence and deceiving the Supreme Court in two of the major cases in its history: two World War II-era rulings that upheld the detention of more than 110,000 Japanese Americans.

Katyal said Tuesday that Charles Fahy, an appointee of President Franklin D. Roosevelt, deliberately hid from the court a report from the Office of Naval Intelligence that concluded the Japanese Americans on the West Coast did not pose a military threat. The report indicated there was no evidence Japanese Americans were disloyal, were acting as spies or were signaling enemy submarines, as some at the time had suggested.

Fahy was defending Roosevelt's Executive Order 9066, which authorized forced removals of Japanese Americans from "military areas" in 1942. The solicitor general, the U.S. government's top courtroom attorney, is viewed as the most important and trusted lawyer to appear before the Supreme Court, and Katyal said he had a "duty of absolute candor in our representation s to the court."

Katyal, 41, who is of Indian American heritage and is the first Asian American to hold the post, said he decided "to set the record straight" Tuesday at a Justice Department event honoring Asian Americans and Pacific Islanders.

He said that two of the government's civilian lawyers had told Fahy it would be "suppression of evidence" to keep the naval intelligence report from the high court.

"What does Fahy do? Nothing," Katyal said.

Instead, Fahy told the justices the government and the military agreed the roundup of Japanese Americans was required as a matter of "military necessity." Roosevelt issued the order on Feb. 19, 1942, about two months after Japan's attack on Pearl Harbor, which plunged the U.S. into World War II.

In 1943, the high court unanimously upheld a curfew imposed on Japanese Americans in the case of Gordon Hirabayashi vs. United States. And in 1944, the court in a 6-3 decision upheld the removal order imposed on Japanese Americans in Fred Korematsu vs. United States. The majority accepted the government's claim that it was a matter of "military urgency."

Scholars and judges have denounced the World War II rulings as among the worst in the court's history, but neither the high court nor the Justice Department had formally admitted they were mistaken — until now.

"It seemed obvious to me we had made a mistake. The duty of candor wasn't met," Katyal said.

Korematsu, who was awarded the Presidential Medal of Freedom by President Clinton, died in Marin County in 2005 at age 86.

On Tuesday, his daughter Karen said she was grateful that Katyal had acknowledged the mistakes of his predecessor.

"It was a remarkable statement he made," she said. "It proves what my father believed all along — that removing the Japanese Americans was wrong and incarcerating them was unconstitutional."

Korematsu was sent to a camp in Utah, one of 10 in the country. California had two, Tule Lake and Manzanar.

Katyal said that last summer he was doing research for several immigration cases when he came upon some ugly, disturbing comments about Asians in 19th century briefs submitted to the Supreme Court. Chinese immigrants were described as "people not suited to our institutions." People from India were described as a "subject race."

He then looked into the history of the World War II internment cases, including documents revealed in the 1980s. Peter Irons, a professor at UC San Diego, had found reports in old government files that showed the U.S. military did not see Japanese Americans as a threat in 1942. His research led to federal court hearings that set aside the convictions of Korematsu and Hirabayashi. Congress later voted to have the nation apologize and pay reparations to those who were wrongly held.

Katyal said he decided it was important to publicly acknowledge the mistakes made in the solicitor general's office. Hiding the truth from the justices, he said, "harmed the court, and it harmed 120,000 Japanese Americans. It harmed our reputation as lawyers and as human beings, and it harmed our commitment to those words on the court's building: Equal Justice Under Law."

Hirabayashi is now 93 and living in Canada. His memory of the World War II years has faded, said his nephew Lane Hirabayashi, a professor of Asian American studies at UCLA. "I know Gordon would be very pleased by this. He didn't know at the time that government prosecutors had distorted evidence. However, he knew in his heart that mass incarceration was unconstitutional," he said.

"I thought it was good and very long overdue," Irons said of Katyal's statement. "This was a deliberate, knowing lie by Fahy to the Supreme Court. For the government's highest counsel to make that statement now is quite noteworthy and admirable."

A year ago, Katyal became the acting Solicitor General when Elena Kagan was nominated to the Supreme Court. He had made a name for himself in legal circles in 2006 when took on the case of Salim Hamdan, who faced a military trial at the U.S. prison at Guantanamo Bay, Cuba. He won in the Supreme Court, which struck down the military commissions because they had not been authorized by Congress.

But that victory in Hamdan vs. Rumsfeld earned him some critics in the Senate — and it may have cost him the chance to win Senate confirmation as solicitor general. This year, President Obama passed over Katyal and nominated Deputy White House Counsel Donald Verrilli Jr. for the post. Katyal said he would step down when the Senate officially confirmed Verrilli.

Here's a good summary of Hirabayashi's landmark case:

During World War II, Gordon Hirabayashi was a 24-year-old senior at the University of Washington - an American citizen by birth - when, as acts of civil disobedience, he defied a curfew imposed on persons of Japanese ancestry and refused to comply with military orders forcing Japanese Americans to leave the West Coast into concentration camps. He appealed his convictions to the U.S. Supreme Court, which, in one of the most infamous cases in American history, held that the curfew order was justified by military necessity and was, therefore, constitutional. A year and a half later, in Korematsu v. United States, the Court relied wholly on its decision in Hirabayashi to uphold the constitutionality of the mass removal of Japanese Americans.

Forty years later, in 1983, represented by a remarkable and dedicated team of lawyers, Mr. Hirabayashi reopened his case, filing a petition for writ of error coram nobis in Seattle,

Continued on Page 51

Sexting and Child Porn Laws
Their Affects on Children

by Randy English

A survey conducted by MTV shows that one-third of young people between the age of 14 and 24 admit that "they've engaged in sexting-related activities

What do you know about Sexting and Child Porn? You may have heard about it on the news, but could it ever affect your life? Well, do you have teenagers? If you do, there is a very good chance these things you consider sick and vile could affect your family.

In today's world where reality TV and the Hollywood baby-sitter known as television rule most homes, children are exposed at an early age to sexually charged images and innuendos. They see sexual acts either being hinted at or if the parents take them to R rated movies, the real thing, from nudity to sexual acts. Today our children are inundated with sexually charged "entertainment" on a daily basis.

What affect does this have on teens and preteens? They see sex and nudity the same way they see foul language and smoking, as just normal. Then, they act on what they have been taught. But more than that, it is at a time in their lives when their sexual drive is awakening naturally and they are eager for experimentation. This leads to exhibitionism, "you show me yours and I'll show you mine." But today it is not done behind the barn. It is done online and on cell phones.

Most of us remember the curiosity of our youthful days. If you would have had devices like kids have today, could you see yourself sending semi-nude pics to your boy/girl friend? Be honest and remember those youthful hormones.

Teens today are much more open about sex than in past generations. Hooking up is the norm, so for today's teens, sexting is tame. If you are familiar with the term "hooking up," it refers to sex without the need of dating, or in many cases even knowing the person at all. It's just a way to kill time for many teens.

How prevalent is sexting? "…girls as young as 10 years old involved in sexting, the sending and receiving of sexual messages and photos, just as 20% of their older peers are known to do…30% of the respondents have already engaged in the practice." CBSNews

These studies count on the teens being honest about their sexting activities. So we are left wondering just how many children were too embarrassed to admit that they have sent or received a sext?

Sexting Laws and Teens.

A teen, under the age of 18 who is caught sexting (Distribution of Child Porn) or anyone (of any age) receiving an under-aged sext (receiving Child Porn) can be charged and face up to 25 years in prison and a lifetime on the Sex Offender Registry. Yes, sexting is very serious. But did you ever think of it as Child Porn? After all when you think of Child Porn you automatically think of a

child being raped by an adult while the adult tapes it. But that is not the case nowadays. Child Porn laws have been expanded to cover even a child taking their own photos and sending them by phone, Internet or other means of broadcasting. Do you think this law is about protecting children? No it never was about protecting children. It is about branding children for life.

If your child were caught sexting or receiving a sext, prosecution is likely. Many parents will take a plea deal thinking that it is best for the child, however they soon find that the Sex Offender Registry is tied into that plea deal. Once your child is placed on the national public registry, there is little chance of ever having a productive life. Work restrictions and residency restrictions will rob them of the freedom that the United States has stood for from its founding. Education is another problem. Registered Sex Offenders, no matter their age, are banned from school property. So how will your child complete their education, this includes many Colleges.

How Can You Protect Your Child.

This part is taken from the SOSEN Sexting Brochure. This brochure can be downloaded at SOSEN.org.

There are several ways to protect your children from the ill-effects of sexting laws.
• Talk with your teens, preteens and tweens.
• Explain in frank terms the legal consequences of sexting.
• Monitor your child's social networking accounts.
• Know what your child is doing online, even if they are older teens.
• Look at the photos on their phone.
• Show your fear and concern!
The reasons why girls engage in these activities
82% say it's to get attention
66% say it's to be "cool"
59% do it because they want to imitate the "popular" girls and 55% say they did it to find a boyfriend."

The next time you see an article about the criminal penalties for sexting, thing about the children's lives that these laws are ruining. It's time to tell the government to stop punishing children, that's the parents responsibility. ■

Washington, seeking vacation of his wartime convictions on the ground that the government, during World War II, had suppressed, altered, and destroyed material evidence relevant to the issue of military necessity. In 1986, the Ninth Circuit, in an opinion authored by Judge Mary Schroeder, vacated both Mr. Hirabayashi's curfew and exclusion convictions on proof of the allegations of governmental misconduct. Hirabayashi v. United States, 828 F.2d 591 (9th Cir. 1987).

So what does this have to do with the subject of the Sex Offender era? Plenty, Congress has been mis-lead and lied to. Now just maybe the lies were not intentional, in any case, the statistical facts have been glaring right under everyone's nose, including Politicians, Legislators, News Media Ratings Whores, Expert Witnesses, Proponents of the Sex Offender Registry, Sexual Abuse Advocates and even people in general so that no one has a valid excuse.

Our own Government, the Department of Justice Statistics, is the one exposing the truth and shattering the myths and fantasies which were sold to our Legislators.

Our Legislators, our Politicians, our Policy Makers need to be aware, just how very expensive it will be for our government, if it is ever discovered and concluded, that Congress was lied to or mislead with false information about Sex Offenders; and they begin to allocate for damages to over 700,000 registrants and their families, it could be that the government will begin to investigate deeper and search out those responsible for this mess.

This kind of mess will always occur when politicians side step standard procedure. There is a reason for checks and balance.

Had the legislators not turned the deaf ear to the governments own statements and established the registry for what it was originally intended, and that is only the most dangerous, it would not be such a dismal and expensive failure. ■

When legislators created the registry, did they forget that registrants had families that would be affected by the thing they created?

Did those legislators stop and think of the harm the registry would cause the spouses and children of registrants?

Now that the truth is out, are legislators concerned about the harm that has been done to these innocent family members? Are they concerned about children, all children, even the children of registrants?

Cut this out and send it to your legislators! Ask them if they are ready to stop harming families.

Movies: Science Fiction

```
T H E S A D F O R B I D D E N P L A N E T
V S S R E S F L A S H G O R D O N N T U R
S I C E I E I S N W E S T W O R L D O E F
P L A P N N B L E I U T E P L C K A G Q T
I E N O E R D B O C E V H O O O O A B U C
D N N O E N U E O P I T G E A C Y N R I A
E T E R R C E P L O A S B A O O E Z L P
R R R T G A O I Y E N R O N V B N B I I M
M U S P T O A E L S N D T C E N Y T O B I
A N C I N O H R R A Y D I E U K E S S R P
N N S H E T T U O S S T E R M R N R S I E
C I I S L D N A N T S R E N M S E A N U E
O N R R Y S A A L A H D E I C N T A R M D
N G A A O M T R T R A E N C I E M H S F S
T E L T S C A N K L E A M L N R D H E Y R
A I O S H G A D B C T C T A A A I A L B A
C H S E T F H D M O I A A T T V R F Y R W
T I R D U N E M R A L T S L E R E T N A R
E S A C A T T A G F X N Y R L H I S O Z A
K R A P C I S S A R U J S I T O N X R I T
E T A G R A T S E M O R D O E D I V T L S
```

ALIEN
BLADE RUNNER
BODY SNATCHERS
BRAZIL
COCOON
CONTACT
CUBE
DARK CITY
DEEP IMPACT
DUNE
EQUILIBRIUM FANTASTIC VOY-
AGE
FLASH GORDON
FLATLINERS
FORBIDDEN PLANET

FRANKENSTEIN
GATTACA
INDEPENDENCE DAY
JURASSIC PARK
LOGAN'S RUN
MAD MAX
METROPOLIS ROBOCOP
SCANNERS
SHIVERS
SILENT RUNNING
SOLARIS
SOYLENT GREEN
SPIDER-MAN
STAR WARS
STARGATE

STARMAN
STARSHIP TROOPERS TERMINATOR
THE ABYSS
THE FLY
THE MATRIX
THEY LIVE
TOTAL RECALL
TRANCERS
TRON
VIDEODROME
WESTWORL

Solution on Page 68

Self Serving Politicians

by Will Bass

How well do public officials uphold their sworn oath to protect the State and Federal Constitutions that require them to protect citizen's individual rights? When legislators are faced with special interest groups pressures that are attempting to strip the rights from small-disfavored groups of American citizens, Legislators that do stand their ground, to protect those small disfavored groups are true American patriots. They realize by doing this they may not be reelected in upcoming elections because of their actions. Honor and integrity and their oath before God to uphold the Constitution, is more important than their personal gain. These people deserve recognition, and deserve to be re-elected.

All of those other legislators simply choose to be swayed from their duty by worries of re-election or fears of loss of personal fame. They also choose this other way in light of important information and data on any relevant issues. They completely ignore that information and also allow themselves to be deterred by any public outcry that is not based on facts, but myths, misconceptions, outright lies and by special interest groups. These special interest groups, seem to purposely distort and twist the truth for their own selfish gains. Through their violation of their oath to God and to the people that they are supposedly to serve, the protection of everyone's liberty is now at stake. Their names will forever go down with others who were only self-serving and selfish, such as Sen. McCarthy and Benedict Arnold. Only time will tell if these legislators and special interest groups will change how selfish they are and return to the tenants of Honor, Truth, and Integrity.■

The Silence of Hundreds of Thousands of Registered Former Sex Offenders Must Indicate the Registry is Working?

by Penn Greene

The resounding silence by the over 750,000 Registered Former Sex Offenders is all that State and Federal Political Leaders need to validate their success in solving a problem that never existed.

Sounds pretty defeatist doesn't it, coming from a Registered Former Sex Offender who has been fighting these mandatory Sex Offender Registry Laws?

But your silence has been devastating to this movement to reform and change the current draconian system from one of an active deprivation of your rights to a proactive movement that truly and effectively prevents all forms of abuse and especially child sexual abuse.

Now I could expound upon the Constitutional issues, case laws, the punitive aspects of the Registry as well as on all the egregious information used to come to the esoteric findings justifying the Registry by those that were, and are politically motivated to do so, but I won't, that's not what this is about.

Not because there are no Constitutional issues, case laws or information and studies that refute and contradict each and every one of the politically motivated reasons for the registry, there are. We have reams and reams of such information. All the reports, studies,

case laws, etc, etc., we have more than any court of law would need to render a verdict in our favor. What we don't have is your voice to raise these issues and present these facts where and when they need to be raised and presented. To press the point that these laws do nothing to protect children and, by all reports and studies, may actually be putting more, and other children, at a greater risk, generating unnecessary collateral damage.

What do you need to do? Get involved. There are many organizations building memberships to give you a voice, join one. Learn the facts and truth behind the laws that are making your life your own "Living Prison" at you and your family's expense. If you can vote, VOTE! And don't stop there, get to know who you are voting for and share with them the information you learn. Get involved in your local and state government, even if it is only appearing at their meetings and hearings. Be that face in the crowd staring them in the eye when they must choose between fact or fiction. And raise your hand, stand up on your own two feet and exercise your "Right To Be Heard"! Because my friends that is about the only right we have left.

Do it today. Tomorrow will be too late for you, your family, for us all. Be a voice of truth and standup for what is right. ■

Would You Consider it Punishment?

By Lynn Gilmore - CEO SOSEN.org

If you were convicted of a single crime many years ago, served your time in jail and finished your probation without re-offense, here in America, would you expect to be able to go on with your life because now your punishment would be over? Yes, of course you would...

But, what if, upon completion of your sentence, your name and photo were posted on a public criminal registry? Would you consider that additional punishment?

Would you consider it punishment for having your employer's name and address publicly displayed with your name and photo?

Would you consider it punishment when you lose that job because of the public registry listing?

Would you consider it punishment when you can't get another job because of the public registry listing?

Would you consider it punishment if you were required to go into your local law enforcement agency and register as a criminal every 90 days, or six or twelve months, even if you had been living offense free in your community for years?

Would you consider it punishment when you're required to pay a registration fee as part of your registration?

Would you consider it punishment when you're required to adhere to a curfew?

Would you consider it punishment when you're required to wear a GPS bracelet?

Would you consider it punishment when you have to pay a fee to wear that GPS bracelet?

Would you consider it punishment when you're not permitted to live where you want because you have residency restrictions placed against you and your family?

Would you consider it punishment when you're required to report to your law enforcement agency every time you travel, move, get a new job or get a new car?

Would you consider it punishment when you're not permitted to use the internet?

Would you consider it punishment when, if you are permitted to use the internet, you must report every email address and user name you use to law enforcement?

Would you consider it punishment when you're not permitted to reside with your family?

Would you consider it punishment when you're not permitted to visit your children at school?

Would you consider it punishment when your children are not permitted to have play dates or sleepovers at your home?

Would you consider it punishment if your family, your spouse and children included, were not allowed to decorate your own home for Halloween?

Would you consider it punishment when your children are bullied and taunted at school because your name and photo was seen on the public registry?

Would you consider it punishment when vigilantes who saw your name and photo on the public registry harass you and your family?

Would you consider it punishment to live with the threat of vigilantes that often take the law into their own hands and murder registered criminals without the fear of facing prison time themselves, because killing a criminal like you has been made justifiable in the eyes of society?

Would you consider it punishment when those vigilantes take the law into their own hands and harass or take the lives of your innocent family members as well?

Would you consider it punishment for having your name and photo posted on a public registry for ten years to life?

Would you consider it punishment to never again be able to live a normal life?

Would you consider it punishment to your innocent family to never be able to live a normal life, or have a decent place to live?

Would you consider it punishment if you were forever treated like a second class citizen who will never, ever, have a second chance at life?

Here in the U.S., society believes that once someone pays their debt to society, serves their time, and complies with and completes parole and probation, they should be allowed to go on with their lives. Any additional punishment is considered unconstitutional. Every American is supposed to be given a second chance, even if you are a murderer, thief, arsonist, drug addict, drug pusher, animal abuser, domestic abuser, etc... That is what makes America so great, right?

Not if you've been convicted of a sex offense.

Isn't that additional punishment? Isn't additional punishment unconstitutional?

Of course, it is.■

View the video at - http://www.youtube.com/watch?v=A1vhE-n2mHM&feature=youtu.be

COMMUNITY NOTIFICATION

by Robert Wolf

I understand your concern for the level I and level II offenders now being placed upon the community notification but one thing I'd like to point out is that even all level III offenders are NOT dangerous. Only a very small percentage of the level III will reoffend. Now the level I and level II offenders begin to understand what the low risk level III offenders have had to go through.

Remember in the early studies done in many cases the only people that they looked at were level III offenders. Some of the studies only looked at rapists. rapists re-offense rate was only in third percentile, with or without treatment. In (1989) Furby, Weinrott, and Blackshaw study was done to find out which treatment programs were the most effective. It is considered to be the most extensive and meticulously analytical. In their findings they stated "there is as yet no evidence that clinical treatment reduces the rate of sex offense. The recidivism rate of treated offenders is not lower than that for untreated offenders; if anything, it tends to be higher." They also showed that untreated and mistreated offenders still reoffend at a lower rates than that of all but one other class of criminals remember the treatment providers are part of the cause of the laws being formed in the first place with such statements as " we had better make laws that say' you are locked for the rest of your life or until you die' because outside of a specialized treatment program for sex offenders, that is the only way to prevent those men from re-offending." (Robert Freman-lango 1983). The ones like " Once a sex offender, always a sex offender." (Maureen Saylor 1981). These treatment by providers have been caught in their lies by all the studies that have come out since then and are now backpedaling trying some way to prove that their programs are beneficial so that they can continue to make money from other people's misery. They have not change their programs, only their tactics in presenting

them.

To give you an idea a humanistic treatment program that was started in 1971 in Santa Clara County California the child sexual abuse treatment program (CSATP) worked with over 3500 offenders and their families totaling over 12,000 individuals over a 15 year period. They worked with people involved in incest and family sexual abuse all of which would be considered a level III. In 1989 this programs re-offense rate was less than 1% and it was found that even without treatment the re-offense rate was in the two percentile (that is a lower re-offense rate than some of the level I and level II offenders have). The primary goal of this treatment was not to stop re-offense but to help the victims and to help keep the families together a goal that was achieved in the 95 percentile again with the offender re-offense rate of less than 1%.

To give you an idea why this treatment program worked this is a quote from their treatment and training manual.

The child sexual abuse treatment program does not rely heavily on the traditional methods of psychotherapy or behavior modification just as the traditional tactics of the criminal justice system are inappropriate for cases the intrafamily sexual abuse so are the medical treatment models based on the curing of disease generally speaking CSATP counseling procedure does not probe the trauma of the past to cure mental afflictions nor does it employ behavior modification to desensitize maladaptive behavior

The goals of CSATP humanistic approach are to enable self-awareness and self-management rather than curing of mental illness what clients can expect from their participation in CSATP is a growing ability to monitor and direct their own life processes and become socially responsible members of society

I wonder if anyone has done a study on the

effects of treatment on the individuals who have been forced into treatment. The study could look into the post traumatic stress disability (PTSD) caused by treatment programs. Most of the treatments are like *A Clock Work Orange* with their procedure verging on torture with their sadistic use of electro shock aversion, foul taste aversion, amyl nitrate conditioning, and aggressive confrontational conditioning. In Robert Balls' book, *Walking on Water*, he states that alternating fear and kindness, such as used in Behavior Modification, is one of the most highly sophisticated tortures used by man. This is a strong and effective way to condition someone's behavior. It also instills high anxiety and destroys self worth. The public has already seen the effects of PTSD in returning vets.

In conclusion I just want to say from my point of view there is no reason why we should even for a moment believe the treatment providers are on our side until such time as they are willing to stand up in court and state the truth that the the vast majority of s will not reoffend with or without treatment and that they the therapists without having extensive long-term one-on-one contact with a person have no way of determining if an individual will reoffend, And even then they cannot do so accurately.∎

Vigilante Receives
Life Sentence

Robert Pascale of Bithlo, Florida will spend the rest of his life in prison for beating to death a 78-year-old man *he thought was a sex offender*. However, the guilty of first-degree murder verdict brought no reaction from the vigilante.

Prosecutor William Jay emphasized during closing arguments that Pascale admitted several times, including in an interview aired on WFTV, that he beat Edwards with a baseball bat. Pascale and his accomplice, Michael Garay, had previously been convicted of violent and criminal acts, however, that information was not allowed to be told to the jury.

Pascale's attorney, Roger Weeden, argued that his client was only guilty of aggravated assault and not premeditated murder.

The question is, why wouldn't it be premeditated since he had targeted a person he thought was a *registered sex offender* and brought along a weapon? The jury came to the appropriate conclusion in this case.

As to the part the registry played in this tragic murder, we do not know, but the hype around sex offender issues surely played a roll.∎

http://www.reformsexoffenderlaws.org/

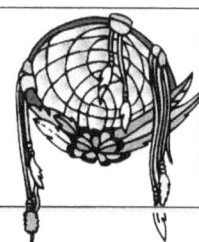

It's No worse Than a Driver's License

by E.D.Tory

I think there's one more thing to this and that is the fact that is in Smith V Doe one of the things that was said was that registration is no more onerous than having a car registration renewed or been required to apply for or renew for a drivers license. The fact that is involved here is that the government is not requiring everyone to have a driver's license or a vehicle registration that owns a form of transportation. Only those that want to use them on city streets and highways. Can you imagine people riding horses along the highway having to have a driver's license and registration and license plate for their horse? Or, how about the same things required for people driving dog sleds? Or for that matter, if everyone that rode in a car or any type of city transportation was told that they had to have a driver's license before they could get into those vehicles? And that they would be arrested for a felony for not having that driver's license and riding any form of transportation. So let's take a look at driver's license registration. This one is important because it is one of the things that are mentioned in the Supreme Court case that sex offender registration is no different than driver's licenses. I know that in some states they have changed the lower age limit of licensed drivers. Originally it was 16 years old, and then during the time, they changed the law, it moved to 18. Did they have to remove the licenses from the people who were under the age of 18? Did they go back to all the people who received their license at the age of 16 and drove for two years before reaching the age of 18 and arrest them for driving without a license and also, does it force everyone who owns a car to have to have a driver's license?

Now let's look at car registration for license plates. Does every car within a given state have to have up-to-date registration and license plates? And if you are in possession of a car, can you be arrested and sent to prison for not registering and putting license plates on your car? This is very strange indeed. I've never seen a license plate on any of the NASCAR cars, or in any demolition derby, and how many farms in this country have old vehicles sitting out behind the barn not to mention all the junkyards. Also what would happen if every junkyard in the country were then told that it had to have registration and up-to-date license plates on every car in their yard? ∎

Political leaders have become salesmen; peddling worthless, freedom stealing laws.
Are you a victim of their propaganda?
Did you buy into their lies?

Those are my principles, and if you don't like them… well, I have others.

Groucho Marx

RSO Advocacy Magazine, it's future and how to use it.

RSO Advocacy is growing quickly and so is our magazine. In future issues you will see continuations of articles started in this issue. We will be doing more interviews. You can expect to see new sections added to the magazine and we hope to hear from you. Send us your comments. Yes, just like on the internet you can comment on our articles and as space provides we will print some of those comments.

At this time we are not offering subscriptions to the magazine.

Ad space is limited so if you are interested in advertising with us, contact us as soon as possible.

On our website located at www.rso-advocacy.org you will find a link to purchase the current issue and back issues, when they become available. We are offering the magazine at a price far below retail to encourage sales.

Ideas for using the magazine:

We feel that RSO Advocacy Magazine is a good tool to use for fund raisers. You can purchase in quantity at a huge discount and sell it at the retail price and you can keep the difference to use towards your groups projects. Remember to add a little for shipping when selling at retail, that will help cover the shipping charge that you pay.

Some people are sending the magazine to those who they feel will benefit the most. For a small cost you can reach influential people with an in-hand, print magazine, that they cannot ignore. But who to send it to? Here are a few suggestions.

Legislators
Sheriff's Office waiting area
Local Law Enforcement
State Law Enforcement
Attorneys
Judges
News Media
Schools and Teachers
Treatment Providers
Prison Libraries
Churches
Hospitals
Even Vigilantes!
And we are sure there are many others who could use a good education.

No matter how you choose to use RSO Advocacy Magazine, you can be sure that you will have a tool that is credible and cannot simply be ignored.

At RSO Advocacy, we are reform, we are organized, we are many and we are growing. If you are not already affiliated with a state group, we invite you to join one today. Also, join SOSEN.org or RSOL or WAR. Make your voice be heard. United we will be heard!

The Problem of Recidivism

by RSO Advocacy Staff

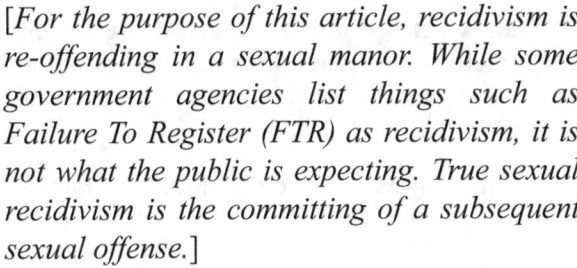

[*For the purpose of this article, recidivism is re-offending in a sexual manor. While some government agencies list things such as Failure To Register (FTR) as recidivism, it is not what the public is expecting. True sexual recidivism is the committing of a subsequent sexual offense.*]

While recidivism among registered offenders is low, it does occur. We cannot and should not deny this problem. We should do our very best to find ways to reduce, or better yet stop recidivism. But how can we do that?

The 'how' is the question that treatment providers have struggled with for decades. Legislators decided to jump in and offer their input in the form of the registry and the many laws dealing with sex offenders. Lately the public has gotten involved and vigilantism has sprang up.

Have any of these things helped with recidivism? Of all of these, only treatment has had any effect on reducing recidivism. The registry and laws pertaining to sex offenses were based on false information, thus the scheme has had little or no effect on recidivism. And while the fear of vigilantism is a powerful force, it has no effect at all on recidivism.

So we are back to therapy. Why does therapy work? Because therapy deals with the real problem the, unbalanced thinking of the offender. The offender is the problem. Cutting that person out of the equation is not the answer. This is why the registry is in effective. The many laws that for the registry form a net that removes the offender from society. It stigmatizes them, demeans them. This is counterproductive to reaching the goal of zero recidivism.

A Better Way

If legislators and the public in general would come to see sexual offending as what it is, a psychological problem, this would be a start. Instead of looking at the crime issue solely and beginning to look at the underlying cause, we could begin to make progress.

I you think about a compulsive thief for a moment. They have a recidivism rate that is one of the highest. No matter how many times they are arrested, they do it again. Some people will argue that this is because the laws are not strict enough. But that is not the true issue. The problem can often be psychological. Kleptomania is the irresistible urge to steal items that you generally don't really need and that usually have little value. Kleptomania (klep-toe-MAY-knee-uh) is a serious mental health disorder that can cause much emotional pain to the one effected and to loved ones and friends. Kleptomania can be treated and thus the cycle can be broken.

The same is true for sexual offending. While some who are misinformed will say that treatment does not work, they are sorely mistaken. William. L. Marshall, Ph.D. said, "For sexual offenders the evidence is mounting that treatment can be effective (Marshall & McGuire, 2003)." He went on to say, "Since sexual offenders display heterogeneity across every aspect of their history, personal characteristics, and sexual interests that have been evaluated (see Marshall, Anderson, & Fernandez, [1999] for a summary of this literature), it makes no sense to treat them all the same. In order to better allocate sexual offenders to treatment programmes that best meet their needs, some pre-treatment assessments are necessary."

So the methodology of treatment is vital. The other aspect of recidivism is the offenders attitude. If the person is unremorseful and resistant to change there is little that anyone can do for them. There are relatively

Continued on Page 65

RSO Advocacy Contract

I Will DO No Harm

Date_____/_____/_____

I _____ acknowledge that my actions of which led to my inclusion on the public registry, were inexcusable. I regret that I caused harm to another person. I am determined to never again harm another person in any way or form, no matter what their age, gender, sexual orientation, color, ethnicity or religious background.

I enter into this contract willingly. From this point on, I will do no harm. I agree to the terms of this contract and enter into the agreement between myself and the other over 750,000 registered sex offenders, with the terms as follow:

If addiction/anger was not involved in the offense that caused you to be included on the public registry, skip to
Section 2.

Addiction Drug/Alcohol

If the offense was contributed to/or exaggerated by addiction to drugs or alcohol, I will seek help. I will remain drug and/or alcohol free, understanding that my addiction is controlling over my life and is harmful to both myself and others.

Anger

If the offense was contributed to/or exaggerated by anger, I will seek help. I will learn my triggers and how to deal with them. I understand that the anger is my problem and not that of others. It is up to me to learn how to control it.

Sex Addiction/Porn Addiction

If the offense was contributed to/or exaggerated by either sex addiction or porn addiction, I will seek help. I will follow the advice of those who can help me. I understand that the problem is bigger than I am, and I need help to overcome the addiction. I understand that the problem is mine and not caused by others.

Section 2

I realize that I will have set backs and wrong desires. For this reason I have asked_____

and _____ and _____ to be my support group. When I feel the desire to fall back into old habits, I will immediately call them and discuss what is causing me to feel this way. I will allow them to help me to remain offense free.

If a members of my support group notice that I am, perhaps, slipping back into my old ways, I will not be angry when they speak to me about it, knowing that I have signed this contact, and that they only bother to say something because they care about me.

Witness _____

Witness _____

Witness _____

The Problem of Recidivism - continued

few registered offenders who fall into this category. In fact most offenders are racked with feelings of worthlessness and regret. Knowing this, legislators should be looking at effective ways to stop sexual recidivism rather than promoting the ineffective tough on crime mentality that the United States has become known for.

At RSO Advocacy we believe that getting the offender involved mentally and emotionally is the key. For this reason we are including our "Contract" in this issue of our magazine. This "Contract" will not be for everyone, but for those that feel it can help them, we encourage you to print it and sign it with as many witnesses as you have available, even if it is only one person that you know and trust. We know that you want to remain offense free and we hope that putting it in writing through this "Contract" will help.

But what if you are alone, with no one to help you? We recommend that you join SOSEN.org. - SOSEN has a members support forum, a safe place for you to talk about what is bothering you and to get the help you need to stay offense free. ■

"One of the great things about books is sometimes there are some fantastic pictures."

-George W. Bush

Don't laugh, some of you voted for him...

Skew Numbers

by Will Bass

If you want to know how to skew numbers within a study. All you have to do is look at Recidivism of Sex Offenders Released from Prison in 1994 (DOJ BOS) where they compare apples and oranges and try to tell you they're all apples.

This is a direct quote from the study;
"Compared to non-sex offenders released from State prisons, released sex offenders were 4 times more likely to be rearrested for a sex crime. Within the first 3 years following their release from prison in 1994, 5.3% (517 of the 9,691) of released sex offenders were rearrested for a sex crime. The rate for the 262,420 released non-sex offenders was lower, 1.3% (3,328 of 262,420)."
But when you actually look at the numbers and do a little research and not taking them at their word. This is what you would find;
In this study, the recidivism rate for rape was 46% and for sexual assault was 41%. Apparently these sex crimes were committed by ex-convicts who had not formerly been convicted of a sex crime, because the same report goes on to say that "within 3 years following their release, 5.3% of sex offenders were re-arrested for another sex crime of that only 3.5% were re-convicted for another sex crime" and only 2% of the rapists were arrested for another rape within the 3-year study period. Therefore of the 46% of ex-convicts who were re-arrested for rape, 44% must not have been previously convicted of a sex crime,but of another type of non sex crime.
The study involved 272,111 inmates. In this study, there were 27 times more non-sex offender ex-convicts than there were released sex-offenders. The ex-convicts who were "not" sex offenders actually committed six times more new sex crimes (517 sex offenders/ 3,326 non-sex offender) than did the released sex offenders. This study showed that 87% of new sex crimes committed by released prisoners in this study were committed by ex-convicts, not by registered sex offenders (USDOJ 2003.)

Fortune Telling

by Will Bass

Human beings have long been in the habit of wanting somebody to have Omniscient Powers to predict the future. When you think of a fortuneteller, you think of a Gypsy-type woman in a dark room with a Swami hat on her head in front of a Crystal Ball. We know in our hearts that these people are really charlatans. Rather because they use those Crystal Balls, Tarot cards, Numerology, our astrological signs, and other "resources" to tell people their "fortunes" and to "see into the future."

Why then should we put any more faith into forensic psychologists who disregard the limits of science by overstating the accuracy of risk assessments and inventing previously unknown disorders to justify preventive detentions? U.S. District Judge Bernard A. Friedman is quoted as saying in the case below, addressing this point, "Even claiming to have same truth telling powers regarding future dangerousness based on unsubstantiated allegations."

This is the case of Markis Revland, a habitual criminal who faced civil detention after serving time for child pornogra-

phy possession, where this same Judge Friedman systematically analyzed and rejected the evidence as failing to meet the government's burden of proof. "Not only did the government fail to show that Revland had a serious mental disorder that put him at high risk of molesting children if released, it even failed to prove that the convict had engaged in any hands-on child molestation in the past." "The court finds that all of the 149 incidents reported by respondent … were the product of his imagination, not actual events." In addition to his conviction for child pornography, Revland had two prior convictions for indecent exposure. However, the most damning evidence against him was his own admissions, made during sex offender treatment at the federal prison in Butner, North Carolina, that he had committed 149 additional incidents of sexual abuse of children of various ages."

The court also agreed and concluded that Revland was desperate to enroll in Butner's treatment program in order to escape the infamous federal prison in Leavenworth, Kansas, where he feared for his life after being

beaten and raped at knifepoint by fellow prisoners. Once at Butner, he felt compelled to fabricate "a long list of sex offenses," lest he be deemed uncooperative and returned to Leavenworth.

"The offenses that he described in great detail were actually implausible, in that he was serving a prior, 10-year prison term for cocaine at around the same time that he claimed to be running around molesting children" The court further stated "The reported incidents were not only too numerous to believe but also recounted – years afterwards – far too precisely, with respondent providing the age of the victim, the time of day … when each offense occurred, and the location where each incident allegedly occurred…. And yet the government offered no evidence to independently verify that any of these incidents occurred or that any of them – even one – ever resulted in investigation or prosecution."

As a group, Butner offenders have confessed to an unusually high number of undetected sex crimes, leading Scientists to suspect that the widely publicized numbers are unreliable. Critics

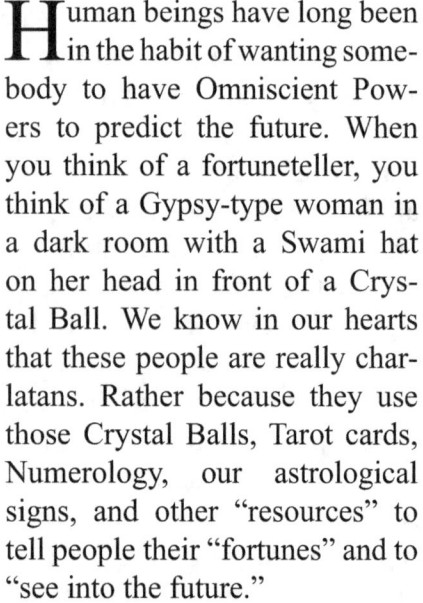

Fortune Telling - Continued

say treatment providers at the federal institution had pressured prisoners to report as many offenses as possible, lest they be accused of not cooperating, and thereby removed from the program.

Finally, the judge rejected the claims of two government psychologists that two so-called actuarial instruments, the Static-99R and the MnSOST-R, showed Revland to be at high risk for recidivism. The Judge said, "the risk assessments by both Dr. Manuel Gutierrez, a Board of Prisons employee, and contracted Psychologist Jeffrey Davis were "particularly unreliable in the present case because they both assumed that [Revland] is a pedophile with numerous 'hands-on' victims, whereas the Court has rejected both of these premises." The judge did concede [that] "the convict met the criteria for antisocial personality disorder." But he found that such a diagnosis was irrelevant:

"The essence of this disorder is that the patient "fails to conform to social norms with respect to lawful behaviors as indicated by repeatedly performing acts that are grounds for arrest." Dr. [Jeffrey] Singer testified, "The vast majority of prison inmates have this disorder, as they are in prison for breaking the law and failing to conform to social norms." Dr. [Joseph] Plaud testified, "There is no documented causal link, in this case or in general, between antisocial personality disorder and sexual dangerousness."

The court credits these experts' opinions. ∎

Anyone who knows history, particularly the history of Europe, will, I think, recognize that the domination of education or of government by any one particular religious faith is never a happy arrangement for the people.

Eleanor Roosevelt

Crossword Fun

ACROSS
1. Collections of anecdotes
5. French for "Friend"
8. Middle East people
12. Do (archaic)
13. Alert
15. South American country
16. As well
17. Motherless or stray calf
18. Russian emperor
19. Believers in one god
22. ___ Saud, creator of the Kingdom of Saudi Arabia
23. Pastry with filling
24. Son of Seth (Bible)
26. Dough for pies
29. Grown up
31. Darkened skin
32. Scorches
34. Young sows
36. Smoky deposit
38. Cephalopod
40. Astronaut ____ Armstrong
41. Layers
43. Beneath
45. Secret agent
46. Demons
48. Pass by
50. Through
51. Force open
52. Mother
54. Acted without restraint
61. Reflexive possessive (contraction)
63. Half diameters
64. French for "Noon"
65. Actress ____ Foch
66. Mixes
67. Electrical engineering society
68. Actor/director ____ Preminger
69. Pig place
70. Parental sibling

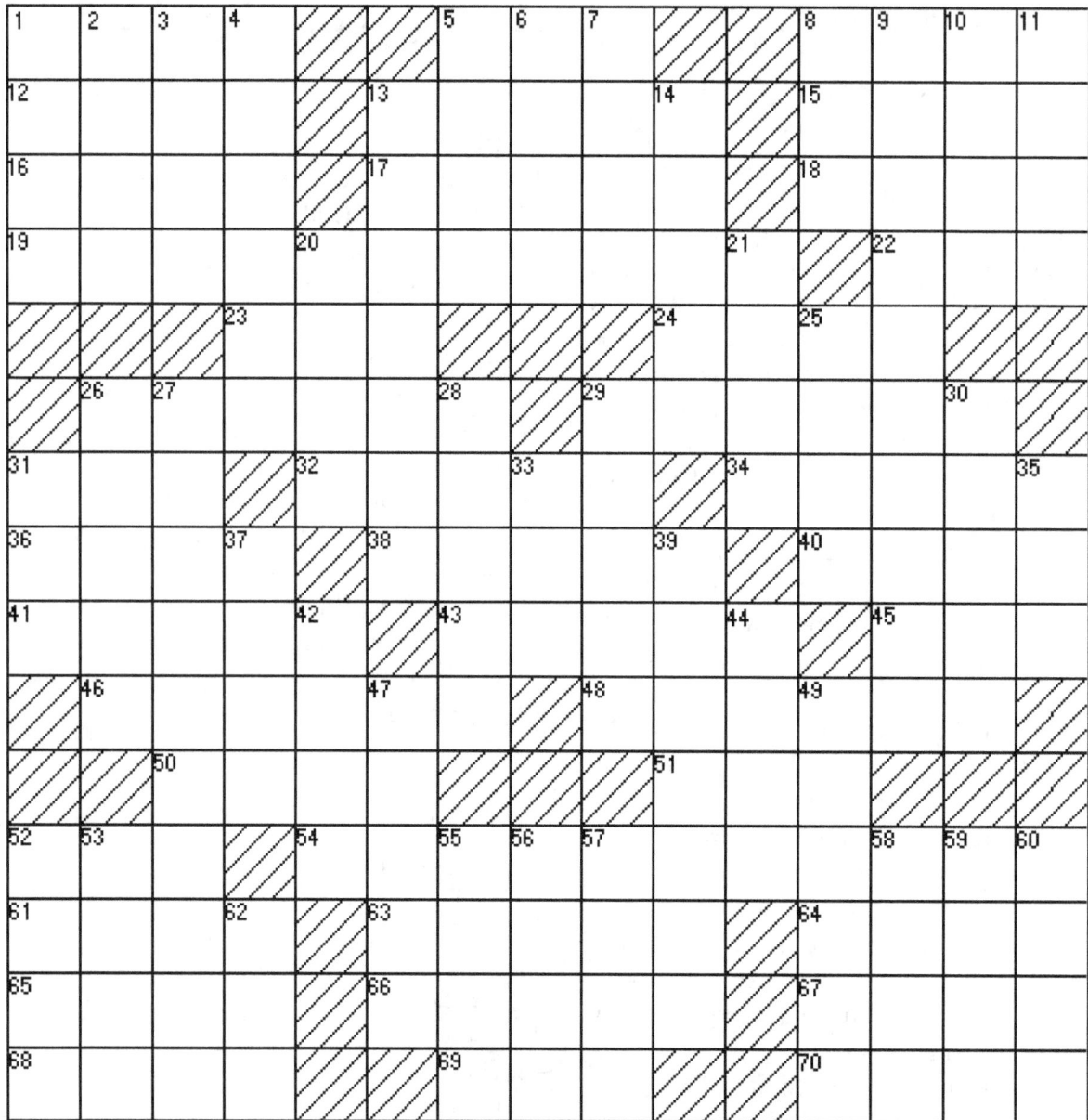

DOWN

1. First man
2. ____ contendre (legal term)
3. Association (abbrev.)
4. Bends over
5. Member of the lily family
6. Wise men
7. Colored part of the eye
8. Capable
9. Without mustering an opposition
10. A Semitic people
11. Consume by fire
13. Sticks to
14. Handed out 20. Various small birds
21. Cozy
25. "Wiseguy" actor Ken ____
26. Small papal coins minted under Paul III
27. Ritual application of oil
28. Mexican Indian tribe

29. Away to one side
30. Stalk-like structure
31. Teaspoon
33. Hurry
35. Clever
37. Technical college (slang)
39. Greek oracles

42. What one does on the web
44. Scarce
47. Prickly clinging seed-cases
49. Blood poisoning from pus
52. One, alone, or single
53. A definite thing
55. Consumes
56. Assemble or modify written material
57. Sinewy
58. Place
59. Paradise

60. Japanese parliament
61. Portuguese for "Saint"

OVERKILL

by Randy English

Some of us expected to see stiff sanctions on Penn State after the Sandusky scandal. Some of us were not at all shocked when the National Collegiate Athletic Association's decision to vacate 112 wins over the past 14 years was announced. Then there is the 60 Million Dollar fine, and the loss of scholarships. While some are in disbelief over this decision, some of us were not surprised at all, we expected it and we also think this is just the beginning.

Some people are asking, "Why make the football players pay for what Sandusky did? Why make the students pay for what school leaders did?"

Is the Penn State fall-out typical?

To answer that question, let's look at three other sexual abuse cases that hit the national news and see what occurred with those cases.

The first is Jacob Wetterling, a boy from St. Joseph, Minnesota who was kidnapped from his hometown on Sunday, October 22, 1989. He was 11 years old when he disappeared. Four months after Jacob's abduction, his parents, Jerry and Patty Wetterling, formed the Jacob Wetterling Foundation, an advocacy group for children's safety. In 1994, the Jacob Wetterling Crimes Against Children and Sexually Violent Offender Registration Act was passed in his honor. It was the first law to institute a state sex-offender registry. Although there is to this day no evidence that a sexual crime was committed this act brought sanctions on everyone convicted of a sex offense, all those who had nothing to do with the Wetterling case.

Next is Megan Kanka, a 7-year-old girl from Hamilton Township, Mercer County, New Jersey. This murder attracted national attention and subsequently led to the introduction of "Megan's Law," which requires law enforcement to disclose details relating to the location of registered sex offenders. Once again a law that targets everyone in a class, not just the one who committed the crime.

Adam John Walsh was a boy who was abducted from a Sears department store at the Hollywood Mall in Hollywood, Florida, on July 27, 1981. Sadly he was later found murdered and decapitated. In fact only his head was found. So no evidence of sexual abuse was present. Adam's death earned national publicity. His story was made into the television movie "Adam," seen by over 38 million people on its original airing.

John Walsh, Adam's father, became an advocate for victims of violent crimes and the host of the television program America's Most Wanted. This spot in the media made it easy for John to push laws against anyone he chose, and once again sex offenders were the targets, although the connection between the death of his child and sex offenders was not there. A convicted "serial killer" (arsonist and serial confessor) Ottis Toole confessed to Adam's murder among hundreds of others he did not commit, but he was never tried for the killing Adam due to loss of evidence and a recanted confession.

With public opinion waning, on December 16, 2008, police announced that the Walsh case was closed as they were satisfied that Toole was the murderer. Toole died of liver failure on September 15. If Toole was the murderer, why did John push for the law passed in memory of his son? The Adam Walsh Child Protection Act is not a law about murdered children. It is a sex offender law. Toole was not, and never was, accused of being a sex offender. He was a murderer. So where, is the sexual connection?

These three examples point to a conclusion that when a sexual abuse case reaches the national level, a reaction will occur. Whether or not that reaction is the correct one, is of no importance at all. The reaction itself seems to be sufficient for the public. They feel better knowing that someone, or many had to pay for a crime that was committed, even if those who are being punished had nothing at all to do with the crime that is bringing the sanctions.

Do we want to live this way? As a nation, do we want to adopt sweeping laws whenever a crime is committed? Once again, we are seeing these kinds of reactions with the Colorado Theater shooting. Some people are advocating for stiffer gun control or even taking away guns all together, as if that would stop someone from committing a crime. So once again on two fronts we are asking, "Why make everyone pay for a crime committed by one person?"∎

YOU CAN'T KEEP A GOOD MAN DOWN

Reggie O'Fender
PART 1 – The Beginning

PART 1

Understand that I am not asking for sympathy or understanding. I am only stating what happened in the following:

In 1994, I was at the top of my game both personally and professionally. I had a loving family and an unusual and lucrative career. I was respected by everyone I knew for who I was. Those who didn't know me personally respected my roles as a husband, father and professional. I was knowledgeable in life and work. I had a liberal arts degree, graduating Magna Cum Laude, which I applied in a technical field. I managed people and products equally well knowing that I could not have one without the other.

Then my life fell apart.

In 1995, I lost the love of my life and about the same time, my company downsized, and I knew I would lose my job. I came close to losing my mind during that time. I withdrew from friends and family. I sought refuge on the Internet. I discovered Internet Porn. Pictures couldn't leave me in pain.

I discovered others with the same addiction. We began surfing the internet and news groups. We would send packets of adult pictures, cartoons and jokes back and forth by email through the rest of 1995 into 1996. Then, one of the people in this email group sent child porn to everyone. I was shocked.

The attachments to the emails were not small. They included dozens of pictures and, at times, small videos. I deleted them immediately. After a couple of emails like this, I blocked the sender. Then, I began receiving the same types of child porn from other members of the group. By this time it was mid 1996 and I was done with this group and all types of porn period! I blocked them all. I even stopped using that email address.

To my surprise, it was to no avail. In late 1996, I came home to three strangers sitting in my home. I asked my house mate who they were and was told they were there to see me. The IDs and badges came out. A point was made to show the guns beneath their jackets. They were FBI agents. I was shocked and confused.

They asked me if I recognized the email address that I had stopped using months before. I told them I did and had not used it for at least four months. They asked me if recognized other email addresses. Some I did from the group mentioned above, others I did not. I asked them what it was all about.

They dropped a bomb on me when I was informed that I was identified as a member of a child porn ring. They said that the email address I said I stopped using was currently active in sending and receiving child porn files. When I told them it wasn't me, they said that they had been monitoring that email account for months and it was active in the past few days. In addition, they had been intercepting the attachments and they were all child pornography. They seized my computer equipment and left. I was not charged or arrested, just devastated.

A few days later I received a call from the Senior FBI agent that had shown up at my door. She told me I had better get a lawyer since they had found a hidden directory that contained "some" child pornography files. I asked her how many files and she said that information would be available after I was indicted. I was shaking with rage and confusion when I hung up on her.

The next day I began my search for a lawyer. I knew that I hadn't done anything wrong. I didn't know that there was a hidden directory on my hard drive. I didn't know there were child pornography files in it. I did know that once I could actually talk to someone higher than the agents, the charges would be dropped. I had faith in the legal system of this great nation. I didn't know what I know now. I didn't know that I was being a fool to believe in Justice. I just didn't know a damn thing about the legal system!■

Look for *"You Cna't Keep a God man Down"* - Part 2 in Our Next Issue

Mortal Slur

by Al Lynne

I was attending a support group a few weeks ago and listening to the participants. One of them in particular was speaking about an incident which occurred at his place of business. He received a call from someone confronting him about a sex offender that works for him. He said he knew him and she replied "... so you allow that pedophile to work for you? ..." Of course she was referring to him. I could tell by what he said and the tones he used that he was really angry. The language was so strong that I will not repeat it here. It was at this point I came to realize that this word can be compared to using a racial slur.

Well, I don't believe it, it took until the 1960's for the Black Americans to finally be free of slavery, and only recently it has become politically incorrect to use the "N-" word. By using that word, it stirs up anger, resentment, hate and could even cause violence. More modern-wise, I consider it to be childish to use hateful or racial slur type words.

We finally begin to get past this kind of immaturity, and now new words begin to appear in our "hate" vocabulary, like "Pedophile" and "Child Molester". Just by using these words will stir up emotion in nearly anyone with ears. Hate groups and vigilantes love to use it because they know it will cause the simple minded to side with them and their agenda of evils.

Even I must contain myself if I am accused of being a Pedophile, so I know how others would feel if they were called as such.

I do not use the word much anymore. It is more of a slang than it is a regular word. It comes from the word "Pedophilia" which is defined by the Diagnostic and Statistical Manual of Mental Disorders (DSM) published by the American Psychiatric Association as someone who has an intense primary and exclusive sexual attraction to pre-pubescent children. It is ironic that people that love to accuse with the word "Pedophile" do not realize that the average age of a Child Sexual Abuser is 14. (see Bureau of Justice Statistics; Sexual Assault Of Young Children As Reported To Law Enforcement: Victim, Incident, And Offender Characteristics pdf pg. eight) They could be making accusations while at the same time their own children could be suffering from the very same condition.

It is a Mental Condition which begins at a very young age and is developed over time. It begins while children are in the curiosity stage of sexuality. Now there is nothing unnatural about sexual curiosity among children. But it is critical that parents monitor the behavior because most of the time, the curiosity will pass. However, if the activity becomes more pronounced and continues, it could become a problem. It becomes a greater problem if an older child interacts sexually with a younger child, for younger children without the natural mental safeguards, are more easily manipulated.

These natural mental safeguards are important and vital for a normal child to develop sexuality without the burden of sexual disorders. When these mental boundaries are chipped away, the child will become less self protective sexually. I call it a "boundary of innocence." It is this innocence that aids in developing a self protective boundary from pre-mature sexuality. Once this boundary is broken down, there is no return to innocence. The fruit has been eaten and therefore banished from the garden of innocence, with absolutely no means of return.

Pedophilia is a serious condition, so is Child Sexual Abuse. Both must be addressed. Pedophilia, in most cases will occur right under our nose as parents and if it is not checked early in life, it becomes an even greater problem if it is carried over as adults. The longer it goes unchecked or untreated, the more difficult it becomes to treat. If it is not treated in adult, there stands a greater chance that someone could become victim of Child Sexual Abuse, and in many cases, it will generate a cycle of sexual abuse, thereby the victim could become the abuser, which has happened many times.

So, consider this before using the words Pedophile and Child Molester, everyone of us was a child at one time. Everyone at one time has had Childhood Sexual Curiosity. None of us were immune to becoming a Child Sexual Abuser. For those that would pursue the opportunity to hate and use these mortal slurs, be advised, you could be mortal slurring your own kin. ◼

RSO Advocacy Magazine Volume 1 September 2012

Registry, Punishment by Default
Arguments for Bills of Attainder

by
Al Lynne
Will Bass

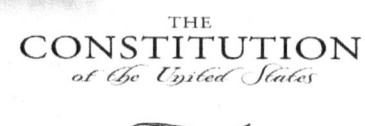

THE
CONSTITUTION
of the United States

The Texas court system has paradoxically started to unravel the justification behind the requirement to register as a sex offender in the state of Texas. The recent case of Michael Arena who was convicted in 1999 at the age of 15 for the sexual abuse of a younger cousin, who has since recanted the accusations, and said the incident never happened.

The Texas Supreme Court sent the case back for re-sentencing, because a prosecution witness provided damaging false testimony at the sentencing. The re-sentencing court took it upon itself to agree to a plea bargain. Lawyers of both defense and prosecution agreed to the Court that Arena would accept a sentence of time served with the stipulation that he would avoid being designated as a sex offender or having to register.

The problem is that the court in so stipulating that Arena does not have to register as a sex offender is essentially admitting that having to register as a sex offender is a form of punishment. Criminal courts can only work within the confines of their authority. If this is the case conversely, a person cannot be put on the registry unless the court so stipulates. If a court has not stipulated for a person to be on the registry at the time of their sentencing, then the offender cannot be added to it by any act of legislation or executive order.

Cases have already been over-turned because it was not stipulated in sentencing of a requirement to register. A number of registrants have already had their convictions over-turned on the grounds that the plea agreement was violated because it was not included in the agreement to be placed on the registry.

That being the case, then perhaps it is time for us to consider the fact that these laws have been passed by the legislative branch of the government against a specific and easily discerned group of people and have set forth the laws in such a way to cause people to have to register and continue to update all their information continuously as well as a required trip to the local Sheriff's office once every three months. To have their information, including their photograph, their address and the vehicles that they drive disseminated on an ongoing basis through the Internet. This quite obviously is a severe handicap on a person's life, liberty, as well as an attack on their reputation. The indication is that this person is dangerous, and incapable of making logical decisions about another person's safety. Quite clearly this was not something that was proven beyond reasonable doubt in any court of law. (Adam Walsh Act)

At this point, the challenge should be made that such legislation is not within the boundaries allowed by the federal Constitution for the executive or the legislative body. To single out a given group of disfavored individuals and remove even one of their constitutional rights or infringes upon those rights is a violation of Bills of Attainder or lesser pains and penalties. Something that the framers of our Constitution held to be repugnant and that the federal or state governments should never be allowed this much power.∎

> **"The Constitution is not an instrument for the government to restrain the people, it is an instrument for the people to restrain the government."**
>
> Patrick Henry

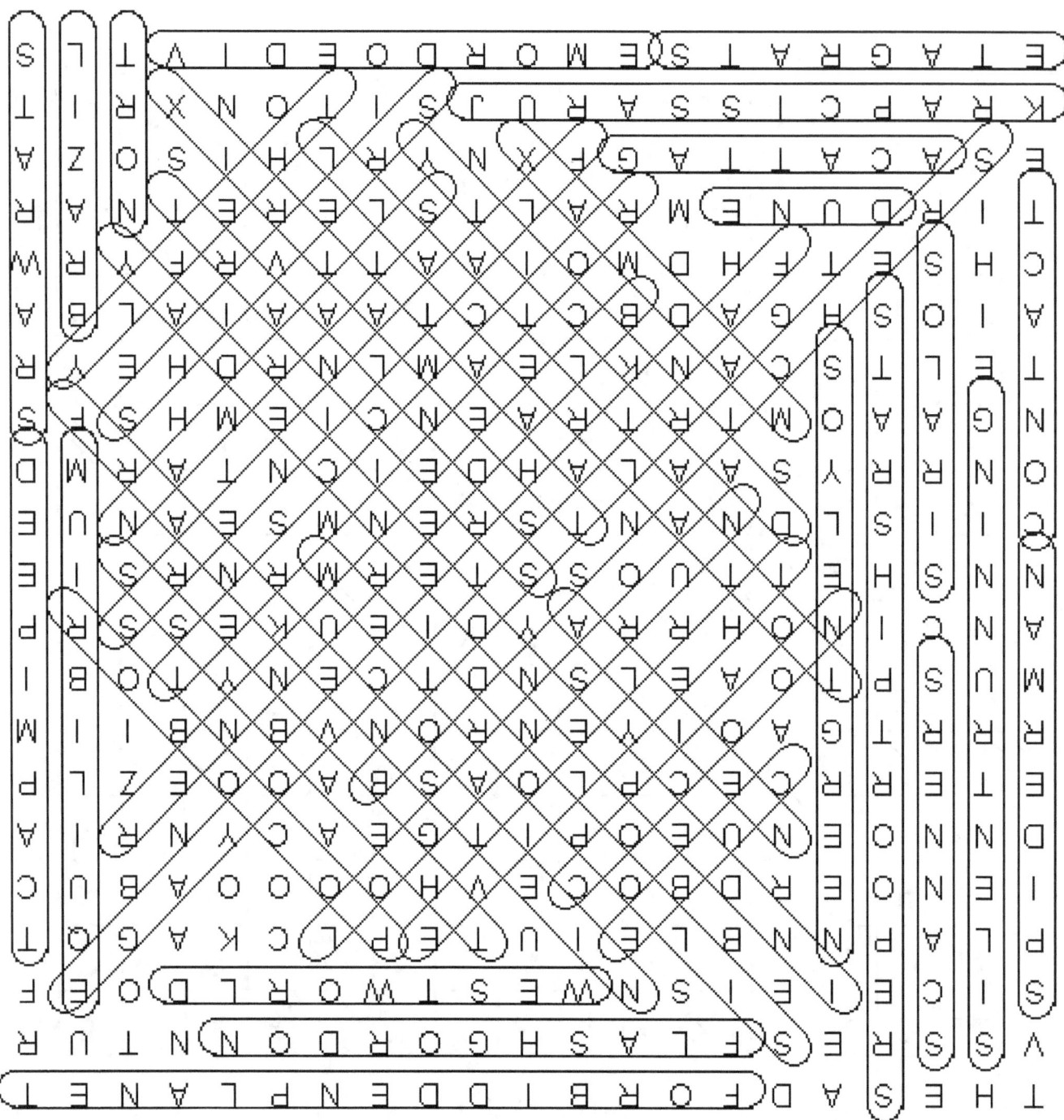